1

This book belongs to:

_____

Aries Daily Horoscope 2023

Aries Daily Horoscope 2023

Aries

2023

JANUARY
MT WT F S S

						1
2	3	4	5	6	7	8
9	10	11	12	13	14	15
16	17	18	19	20	21	22
23	24	25	26	27	28	29
30	31					

FEBRUARY
MT WT F S S

		1	2	3	4	5
6	7	8	9	10	11	12
13	14	15	16	17	18	19
20	21	22	23	24	25	26
27	28					

MARCH
MT WT F S S

		1	2	3	4	5
6	7	8	9	10	11	12
13	14	15	16	17	18	19
20	21	22	23	24	25	26
27	28	29	30	31		

APRIL
MT WT F S S

					1	2
3	4	5	6	7	8	9
10	11	12	13	14	15	16
17	18	19	20	21	22	23
24	25	26	27	28	29	30

MAY
MT WT F S S

1	2	3	4	5	6	7
8	9	10	11	12	13	14
15	16	17	18	19	20	21
22	23	24	25	26	27	28
29	30	31				

JUNE
MT WT F S S

			1	2	3	4
5	6	7	8	9	10	11
12	13	14	15	16	17	18
19	20	21	22	23	24	25
26	27	28	29	30		

JULY
MT WT F S S

					1	2
3	4	5	6	7	8	9
10	11	12	13	14	15	16
17	18	19	20	21	22	23
24	25	26	27	28	29	30
31						

AUGUST
MT WT F S S

	1	2	3	4	5	6
7	8	9	10	11	12	13
14	15	16	17	18	19	20
21	22	23	24	25	26	27
28	29	30	31			

SEPTEMBER
MT WT F S S

				1	2	3
4	5	6	7	8	9	10
11	12	13	14	15	16	17
18	19	20	21	22	23	24
25	26	27	28	29	30	

OCTOBER
MT WT F S S

						1
2	3	4	5	6	7	8
9	10	11	12	13	14	15
16	17	18	19	20	21	22
23	24	25	26	27	28	29
30	31					

NOVEMBER
MT WT F S S

		1	2	3	4	5
6	7	8	9	10	11	12
13	14	15	16	17	18	19
20	21	22	23	24	25	26
27	28	29	30			

DECEMBER
MT WT F S S

				1	2	3
4	5	6	7	8	9	10
11	12	13	14	15	16	17
18	19	20	21	22	23	24
25	26	27	28	29	30	31

2023 AT A GLANCE

Eclipses

Hybrid Solar – April 20th

Penumbral Lunar – May 5th

Annular Solar – October 14th

Partial Lunar -October 28th

Equinoxes and Solstices

Spring - March 20th 21:25

Summer - June 21st 14:52

Fall – September 23rd 06:50

Winter – December 22nd 03:28

Mercury Retrogrades

December 29th, 2022 Capricorn - January 18th Capricorn

April 21st Taurus – May 15th Taurus

August 23rd Virgo – September 15th Virgo

December 13th Capricorn - January 2nd, 2024 Sagittarius

2023 FULL MOONS

Wolf Moon: January 6th, 23:09

Snow Moon: February 5th, 18:30

Worm Moon March 7th, 12:40

Pink Moon: April 6th, 4:37

Flower Moon: May 5th, 17:34

Strawberry Moon: June 4th, 3:42

Buck Moon: July 3rd, 11:40

Sturgeon Moon: August 1st, 18:32

Blue Moon: August 31st, 1:36

Corn, Harvest Moon: September 29th, 9:58

Hunters Moon: October 28th, 20:23

Beaver Moon: November 27th, 9:16

Cold Moon: December 27th, 0:34

2023 INGRESSES

Mars Ingresses

Mar 25, 2023, 11:36	Mars enters Cancer
May 20, 2023, 15:24	Mars enters Leo
Jul 10, 2023, 11:34	Mars enters Virgo
Aug 27, 2023, 13:15	Mars enters Libra
Oct 12, 2023, 3:39	Mars enters Scorpio
Nov 24, 2023, 10:10	Mars enters Sagittarius

Venus Ingresses

Jan 3, 2023, 2:06	Venus enters Aquarius
Jan 27, 2023, 2:29	Venus enters Pisces
Feb 20, 2023, 7:52	Venus enters Aries
Mar 16, 2023, 22:31	Venus enters Taurus
Apr 11, 2023, 4:43	Venus enters Gemini
May 7, 2023, 14:20	Venus enters Cancer
Jun 5, 2023, 13:42	Venus enters Leo
Oct 9, 2023, 1:06	Venus enters Virgo
Nov 8, 2023, 9:27	Venus enters Libra
Dec 4, 2023, 18:48	Venus enters Scorpio
Dec 29, 2023, 20:21	Venus enters Sagittarius

Mercury Ingresses

Feb 11, 2023, 11:22	Mercury enters Aquarius
Mar 2, 2023, 22:49	Mercury enters Pisces
Mar 19, 2023, 04:22	Mercury enters Aries
Apr 3, 2023, 16:20	Mercury enters Taurus
Jun 11, 2023, 10:24	Mercury enters Gemini
Jun 27, 2023, 0:22	Mercury enters Cancer
Jul 11, 2023, 4:09	Mercury enters Leo
Jul 28, 2023, 21:29	Mercury enters Virgo
Oct 5, 2023, 0:06	Mercury enters Libra
Oct 22, 2023, 6:46	Mercury enters Scorpio
Nov 10, 2023, 6:22	Mercury enters Sagittarius
Dec 1, 2023, 14:29	Mercury enters Capricorn

Slower Moving Ingresses

Mar 7, 2023, 13:03	Saturn enters Pisces
Mar 23, 2023, 8:42	Pluto enters Aquarius
May 16, 2023, 17:01	Jupiter enters Taurus

The Moon Phases

- New Moon (Dark Moon)
- Waxing Crescent Moon
- First Quarter Moon
- Waxing Gibbous Moon
- Full Moon
- Waning Gibbous (Disseminating) Moon
- Third (Last/Reconciling) Quarter Moon
- Waning Crescent (Balsamic) Moon

New Moon (Dark Moon)

The New Moon reveals what hides beyond the realm of everyday circumstances. It creates space to focus on contemplation and the gathering of wisdom. It is the beginning of the moon cycles. It is a time for plotting your course and planning for the future. It does let you unearth new possibilities when you tap into the wisdom of what is flying under the radar. You can embrace positivity, change, and adaptability. Harness the New Moon's power to set the stage for developing your trailblazing ideas. It is a Moon phase for hatching plans for nurturing ideas. Creativity is quickening; thoughts are flexible and innovative. Epiphanies are prevalent during this time.

Waxing Crescent Moon

It is the Moon's first step forward on her journey towards fullness. Change is in the air, it can feel challenging to see the path ahead, yet something is tempting you forward. Excitement and inspiration are in the air. It epitomizes a willingness to be open to change and grow your world. This Moon often brings surprises, good news, seed money, and secret information. This Moon brings opportunities that are a catalyst for change. It tempts the debut of wild ideas and goals. It catapults you towards growth and often brings a breakthrough that sweeps in and demands your attention. Changes in the air inspiration weave the threads of manifestation around your awareness.

First Quarter Moon

The First Quarter Moon is when exactly half of the Moon is shining. It signifies that action is ready to be taken. You face a crossroads; decisive action clears the path. You cut through indecisiveness and make your way forward. There is a sense of something growing during this phase. Your creativity nourishes the seeds you planted. As you reflect on this journey, you draw equilibrium and balance the First Quarter Moon's energy before tipping the scales in your favor. You feel a sense of accomplishment of having made progress on your journey, yet, there is still a long way to go. Pause, take time to contemplate the path ahead, and begin to nurture your sense of perseverance and grit as things have a ways to go.

Waxing Gibbous Moon

Your plans are growing; the devil is in the detail; a meticulous approach lets you achieve the highest result. You may find a boost arrives and gives a shot of can-do energy. It connects you with new information about the path ahead. The Moon is growing, as is your creativity, inspiration, and focus. It is also a time of essential adjustments, streamlining, evaluating goals, and plotting your course towards the final destination. Success is within reach; a final push will get you through. The wind is beneath your wings, a conclusion within reach, and you have the tools at your disposal to achieve your vision.

Full Moon

The Full Moon is when you often reach a successful conclusion. It does bring a bounty that adds to your harvest. Something unexpected often unfolds that transforms your experience. It catches you by surprise, a breath of fresh air; it is a magical time that lets you appreciate what your work has achieved. It is time for communication and sharing thoughts and ideas. It often brings a revelation eliminating new information. The path clears, and you release doubt, anxiety, and tension. It is a therapeutic and healing time that lets you release old energy positively and supportively.

Waning Gibbous (Disseminating) Moon

The Waning gibbous Moon is perfect for release; it allows you to cut away from areas that hold back true potential. You may feel drained as you have worked hard, journeyed long, and are now creating space to return and complete the cycle. It does see tools arrive to support and nourish your spirit. Creating space to channel your energy effectively and cutting away outworn regions creates an environment that lets your ideas and efforts bloom. It is a healing time, a time of acceptance that things move forward towards completing a cycle. This the casting off the outworn, the debris that accumulates over the lunar month is a vital cleansing that clears space and resolves complex emotions that may cling to your energy if not addressed.

Third (Last/Reconciling) Quarter Moon

This Moon is about stabilizing your foundations. There is uncertainty shifting sands; as change surrounds your life, take time to be mindful of drawing balance into your world. It is the perfect time to reconnect with simple past times and hobbies. Securing and tethering your energy does build a stable foundation from which to grow your world. It is time to take stock and balance areas of your life. Consolidating your power by nurturing your inner child lets you embrace a chapter to focus on the areas that bring you joy. It is not time to advance or acquire new goals. It's a restful phase that speaks of simple pastimes that nurture your spirit.

Waning Crescent (Balsamic) Moon

The Waning Crescent Moon completes the cycle; this Moon finishes the set. It lets you tie up loose ends, finish the finer details, and essentially creates space for new inspiration to flow into your world once the cycle begins again. The word balsamic speaks of healing and attending to areas that feel raw or sensitive. It is a mystical phase that reconnects you to the cycle of life. As the Moon dies away, you can move away from areas that feel best left behind. Focusing on healing, meditation, self-care, and nurturing one's spirit is essential during this Moon phase.

The Full Moon: How it can affect your star sign

The Full Moon shines a light on areas that seek adjustment or healing in your life. Here are three aspects that may affect your star sign.

The first aspect is the healing qualities provided by the Full Moon.

The Full Moon is a time to bring awareness into your spirit of the areas that seek resolution or adjustment. Over time, the past can create emotional blockages in your life. The Full Moon forms a sacred space to process sensitive emotions and release the past's hold on your spirit.

The second aspect is the effect the Full Moon has on emotions.

This lunar vibration brings awareness to your spirit of how your emotions affect your daily life. When the Moon is complete, your emotional awareness magnifies, and you feel things more intensely in your everyday life.

The third aspect is meditative, reflective, and inward.

The Full Moon brings a chance to go over inner terrain and connect with your intuition. She shines a light on areas that hold the most significant meaning in your life. This effect has a powerful impact on creativity, planning, and future life direction. Tuning in and listening to your gut instincts helps you strip away from areas that only cloud judgment and muddy your awareness.

Aries: Healing your inner child will bring benefits into your daily life. When ambition runs high, you lose touch with childhood innocence and the more specific aspects of life.

I use the 24-hour clock/military time.
Time set to Coordinated Universal Time Zone (UT±0)

I've noted Meteor Showers on the date they peak.

January

Sun	Mon	Tue	Wed	Thu	Fri	Sat
1	2	3	4	5	6	7
8	9	10	11	12	13	14
15	16	17	18	19	20	21
22	23	24	25	26	27	28
29	30	31				

New Moon

WOLF MOON

30 Friday

31 Saturday

1 Sunday ~ New Year's Day, Venus conjunct Pluto 5:24

Venus, the ruler of love, offers an abundant landscape when conjunct with Pluto. The energy of transformation surrounds your life, enabling you to advance your romantic life. You lift the lid on an expansive journey that heightens socializing opportunities. It does see an influx of energy that lets you brew a blend of manifestation that is potent and innovative.

2 Monday ~ Mercury sextile Neptune 6:53

This sextile attracts free-flowing and creative ideas that help you place the cherry on top of this year's plans and aspirations. Life holds a refreshing change. It brings movement and discovery. When you realize the possibilities are impressive, it does broaden your perception of what is achievable when you set your mind to developing your interests. It involves reshaping goals, life picks up momentum, and you enter a busy and active environment.

3 Tuesday ~ Venus ingress Aquarius 2:06, Quadrantids Meteors runs Jan 1st – 5th

The joy and abundance you resonate with reflect in your life. An area you get involved with initiates a wave of transformation. This journey elevates your life on several levels, and you are pleased with the results achieved. You are entering a changing cycle. Being open to new possibilities and avenues of growth help you achieve your highest outcome. You soon unpack a colorful chapter that brings new opportunities to light.

4 Wednesday ~ Venus sextile Jupiter 9:07

This sextile attracts warm and abundant energy into your social life. A dash of luck and good fortune combined with enriching conversations improve social bonds in your life. Moving in alignment with your heart will be the best move forward. It encourages expansion in your social life. There are opportunities ahead that bring connection and kinship into focus.

5 Thursday ~ Sun trine Uranus 16:43

This Sun trine Uranus transit brings positive change and excitement flowing into your world. A transformational aspect brings a path that offers rejuvenation. You harness a sense of vitality and freedom. You can step out on a journey that involves developing your passion projects. It brings a strong emphasis on improving the foundations in your life. You connect with someone who offers insightful advice and a refreshing viewpoint.

6 Friday ~ Wolf Full Moon in Cancer 23:09

You face a crossroads; a firm decision ahead brings a path that offers abundance. Everything does turn out for the best. You teeter on the precipice of change. Harnessing the strength of spirit lets you expand your horizons; it brings the power of peace into your foundations. It does have a direct effect on bringing potential into your world.

7 Saturday ~ Sun Conjunct Mercury 12:56

This conjunct bodes well for communication. Rising prospects draw insightful conversations. It does see news arrives to tempt you out in your broader social circle. It brings exchanges that facilitate growth. Sharing ideas and thoughts with others marks an essential new chapter that lets you greet the future with an open spirit. It does see a theme of abundance is ready to emerge, and an enriching sense of connection lights the path forward.

8 Sunday ~ Mercury trine Uranus 23:22

Mercury forming a trine with Uranus brings flashes of insight; expect an epiphany as brilliance surrounds your thought processes today. It's about looking at your life and your future goals. Exploring the potential that swirls around your environment lets you be a tourist in your own experience. You gain a broader perception of your life and can begin to see potential pitfalls and exciting possibilities.

9 Monday ~ Venus trine Mars 15:21

This week, Venus trine Mars raises your energy and brings a vibrant passion for life. You can embrace the changes ahead. It does seem you get exciting news regarding your social life. It brings a new attitude, and you can see things from a refreshing perspective. You build a rapport with people who are on the same wavelength. It does feed your confidence; it brings a chapter that revolutionizes how you communicate and express yourself to others.

10 Tuesday

New energy is coming that rekindles your vitality. It does have you keen to explore a broader range of potential. Expanding your horizons gives you the green light to start an endeavor that makes a splash when it touches down in your life soon. It does take you towards learning an area of interest. Crafting your skills advances your abilities and, ultimately, broadens your options.

11 Wednesday

Being flexible and adaptable helps you achieve a sound clip of progress. It is an area that offers room to increase your bottom line and provide you with extra security. Growing your talents lets you expand your life outwardly. The pace quickens as you launch towards advancement. Weeding out distractions helps you work efficiently and effectively to achieve a higher level of productivity.

12 Thursday ~ Mars turns direct 20:54

With the planet Mars moving forward, your energy, passion, and drive return full force. Work-related opportunities crop up to inspire you. It does involve a degree of research and planning. Exploring options lets you blaze a trail towards rising prospects. Imaginative and creative possibilities nurture inspiration. The path ahead speeds up and draws a time of expansion. Things are moving along for your working life. It seals the deal on a productive chapter ahead.

13 Friday ~ Sun sextile Neptune 14:11

Resources and support help you get busy manifesting your vision. The Sun sextile with Neptune is the stuff you make dreams from, and you soon get busy crafting your vision for future growth. A golden opportunity flows into your life. It does see you prioritize an aspect that offers a rich reward. Streamlining your efforts helps you cut away from areas that limit progress. It does see you enjoying a fast-paced and hectic environment ahead.

14 Saturday

Adventure and excitement figure prominently in the chapter ahead. It does see a social environment that connects you with others. It is an expressive, creative, and enriching time. New potential sweeps in with some significant changes in tow. It helps you kick off a path that sees life becoming energizing and active. You can get busy and embrace this social environment as it shines a light on connecting with friends.

15 Sunday ~ Venus square Uranus 1:21, Last Quarter Moon in Libra 2:12

A Venus Uranus square creates a need to balance and harmonize interpersonal bonds while honoring your need for freedom and expression. You can free your imagination, remove the boundaries and doubt, and release limitations. Your intuition is guiding a process of increasing your world. Taking time to check in with your inner voice helps you move forward in alignment with your vision. You gain a fresh perspective into an area that may have felt limited.

16 Monday ~ Martin Luther King Day

A piece of news offers a lucky break that opens a fortunate trend. You hear upbeat information on the grapevine. It brings a chance to engage with your social circle later in the week. Indeed, an emphasis on improving circumstances lights a path towards increasing happiness. Nurturing social connections helps you break fresh ground. It brings a busy time of advancing life forward and engaging with a broader world of potential.

17 Tuesday

Life picks up steam, broadening horizons lets you hit your stride and achieve a stellar performance today. A lighter energy flow helps you achieve steady growth as it lets you work smarter, not harder today. Your concentration is sharp and brings focus and discipline to the tasks at hand. It brings balance and stability into focus. Untapped strengths are soon given an avenue for expression in the workplace.

18 Wednesday ~ Mercury turns direct 13:12

Mercury is the messenger planet of communication, collaboration, and creative expression. Life becomes more manageable and flows more easily during Mercury's direct phase. You discover the pace and rhythm of life pick up, bringing social activities that draw movement and discovery. It's a clear message that things are on the move for your social life.

19 Thursday

There's an opportunity to come knocking soon. It does bring an offer of expansion that takes you beyond your current comfort level. As you understand the path ahead, you push back barriers and take the steps necessary to achieve the highest result. Advancement is looming that has you opening the door and kicking off an exciting chapter towards your vision. It is an energizing time that inspires growth.

20 Friday ~ Sun ingress Aquarius 8:26

As you take stock and reflect on the changes that swirl around your life, you unearth innovative possibilities that nurture creativity. It brings solutions that draw balance and harmony into your life. The climate ripens with unique avenues that tempt you forward. It flings open a sunny aspect that connects you with inspiration—lighter energy draws, supportive discussions, social engagement, and relaxing downtime shared with friends.

21 Saturday ~ New Moon in Aquarius 20:54

You head towards a time that reinvigorates and renews your energy. It lifts flagging spirits as it connects you with a path that grows your abilities. It brings a creative undertaking that puts your skills front and center. Using your talents to develop curious sidelines opens your book of life to a new page that initiates refreshing prospects. Creating and working with your skillset shines your abilities and enables you to share your gifts with a broader audience.

22 Sunday ~ Venus conjunct Saturn 22:12, Uranus turns direct 23:23
Chinese New Year (Rabbit)

The Chinese New Year heralds good luck and fortune. Rabbits are a symbol of growth and fertility. Ideas planted in fertile terrain will get a chance to blossom and grow. Setting aspirations in place lets you plan and move forward correctly. A life transition is coming that takes you towards a highly creative phase. It does bring opportunities to mingle with others in your community.

23 Monday

It is a great time to map new goals and endeavors. Transformation sweeps in to encourage expansion. A new dynamic cycle becomes a dominant feature over the coming months. You can take your aspirations to the next level by exploring a broad range of possibilities. It offers room to progress your skills and expand your knowledge base. Working with your abilities draws a pleasing result for your life.

24 Tuesday

There is an opportunity coming up to switch things up and immerse yourself in a new role. It lights a path to a prosperous time of transformation. It brings a new chapter to your working life that involves learning the ropes of a new area. It brings the room to grow into a meaningful path of progress and stability for your working life. Exploring your options helps you snag a sweet deal and come up with trumps.

25 Wednesday ~ Sun sextile Jupiter 1:30

In sextile with Jupiter, the Sun attracts a restless vibe that has you yearning to expand your life outwardly. Good fortune lights a shimmering path forward that has you eager to set out on a new journey. It highlights an approach that blesses your life with new options as it helps you grow your circle of friends. It is a time of adventure and expansion that lets you shed your conservative side and embrace a diverse path forward.

26 Thursday

As you head down the river of life, there will always be a few rocks on the riverbed that create turbulence. Learning how to navigate downstream towards calmer waters helps grow your experience. It brings skills and abilities that enable you to balance life's ups and downs without becoming adrift. Taking time to process and integrate changes in your life draws a stable foundation.

27 Friday ~ Venus ingress Pisces 2:29

Venus slides into your twelfth house of endings, healing, and closure. The universe is sending a sign that it's time to shut the door on a past romantic situation that may be clinging to your energy. Resolving sensitive areas and healing troublesome energy is therapeutic. It nurtures more stability and grounded foundations in your love life. It brings a clean slate of potential into your romantic life that leaves you feeling renewed and recharged.

28 Saturday ~ First Quarter Moon in Taurus 15:19

Setting future intentions helps you chase a vision for future growth. It sows the seeds of inspiration that bring new prospects flowing into your social life. It kicks off an exciting chapter that offers opportunities to mingle and network. New foundations ahead get an active time of nurturing interpersonal bonds. It helps you find your groove in a more social landscape.

29 Sunday

Taking time to reboot and center your energy creates space for balance. You begin to see the options in your world from a new perspective. It helps manifest goals as you launch towards a direction that aligns with your chosen path. It does see life ahead becomes active and inspiring; this brings a joyful chapter. Luminescent potential supports a phase of expansion. Freedom and adventure are on the horizon, tempting you forward.

FEBRUARY

Sun	Mon	Tue	Wed	Thu	Fri	Sat
			1	2	3	4
5	6	7	8	9	10	11
12	13	14	15	16	17	18
19	20	21	22	23	24	25
26	27	28				

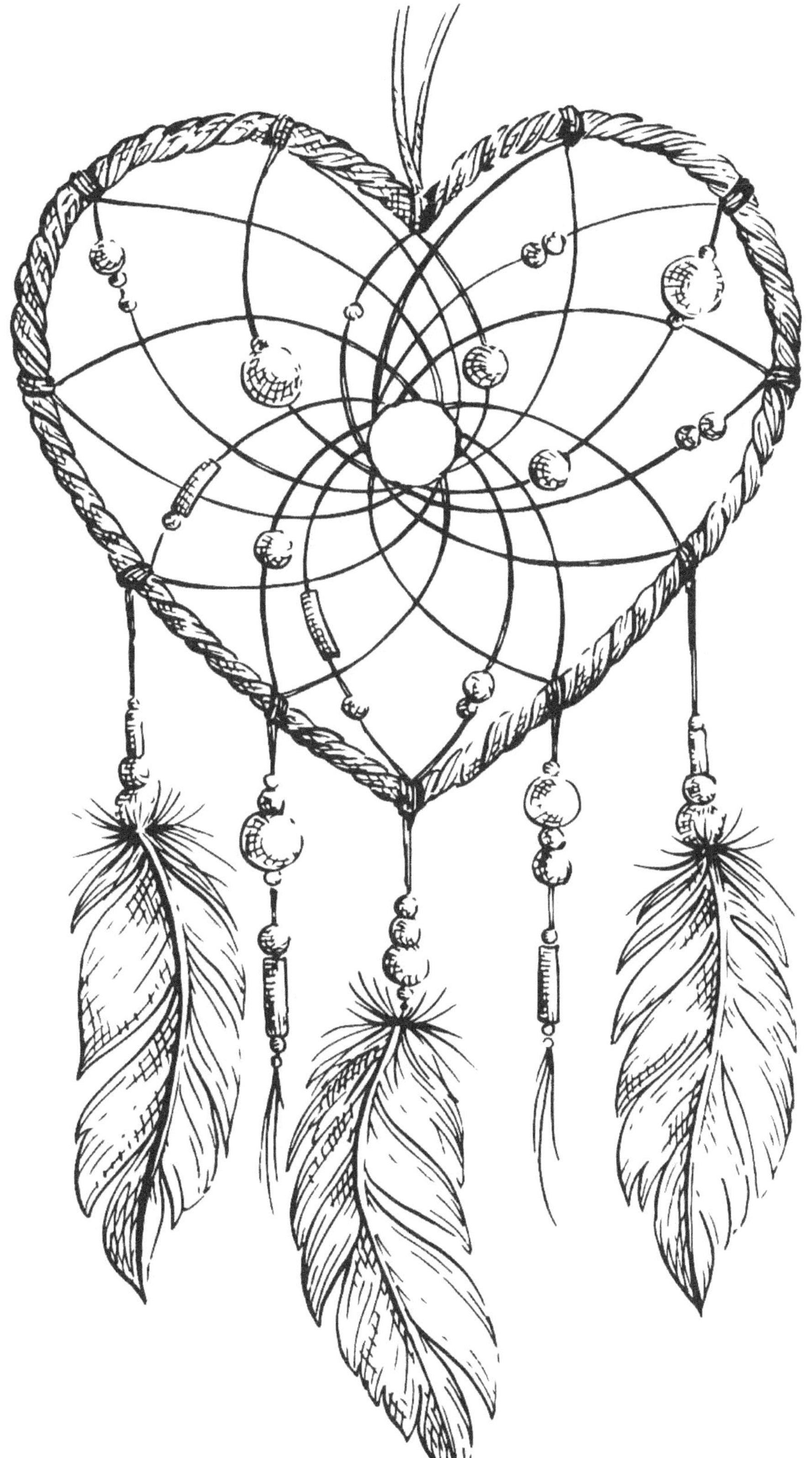

New Moon

SNOW MOON

30 Monday ~ Sun trine Mars 1:45, Mercury trine Uranus 2:17
Mercury at Greatest Eastern Elongation: 25.0°W

Exciting changes ahead draw lightness into your world. It brings a chance to nurture your talents and evolve your gifts. Expansive horizons bring curious news that hits a sweet note in your life. It does let you brew up exciting possibilities as you nurture the magic and creativity that seeks expression in your world. Focusing on building grounded foundations brings new options into your life.

31 Tuesday

Surprise news ahead charms your life with new possibilities. It lets you make headway on improving the building blocks of your world as it ramps up the potential possible in your life. Change flows into your world as you discover an option that inspires growth and evolution. You soon get busy developing the path ahead and embrace an active and lively time of transition.

1 Wednesday ~ Imbolc

Focusing on your journey is imperative in removing the drama from your life. It helps unscramble mixed signals that cause distraction and confusion. Getting all the facts before embarking on a course of action nurtures balance and stability in your world. It lights a path of self-expression that amplifies the success rate in your life.

2 Thursday~ Groundhog Day

You unwrap a new cycle soon that leads to a bold chapter. It lets you embark on a journey that sparks spontaneous adventures with someone who inspires your mind. It brings a fantastic soul journey that offers room to grow into a meaningful area. It has you feeling hopeful and inspired about future possibilities. It brings a productive chapter that gives space to grow and prosper.

3 Friday

The wheels are in motion to improve your circumstances. New possibilities trickle in at first but curious options soon become a flood of potential that draws lighter energy into your life. It lets you focus on creating a journey that gives you a chance to elevate your abilities and grow your talents. You glide into a chapter of possibility that acts as a catalyst for change. It corresponds with developing endeavors as you embark on a mission to grow your life outwardly.

4 Saturday ~ Sun square Uranus 2:50

This positive square offers rising creativity that cultivates a new approach. You soon hone in on new possibilities that inspire growth and progression in your life. Curious changes ahead bring improvement into your world. It rebalances energy as it draws stability into your home life. It creates foundations that offer room to build balance; you enjoy a calming and settled environment that creates space for developing new projects and endeavors. It helps you create the kind of change you seek as it offers excitement around a burgeoning creative enterprise.

5 Sunday ~ Venus square Mars 3:28, Snow Full Moon in Leo 18:30

This square can cause challenges as a difference of opinion fosters tension and conflict. Being flexible, understanding, and adaptive will help harmonize bonds and limit the disruption caused by Venus facing Mars at a harsh angle. Being willing to compromise will improve the foundations and limit the disruption in your life.

6 Monday ~ Mercury sextile Neptune 18:27

Rational thinking and dreams align in this sextile. You see rising creativity and analytical thinking promoting epiphanies that count. This cosmic alignment helps your dreams become a reality as structured backing behind your vision offers tangible results. A lighter flow of energy sparks creative ideas as you diverge from well-worn routines and engage in expanding your life in a new direction.

7 Tuesday

You soon hone in on new possibilities that inspire growth and offer progression in your life. Curious changes ahead bring an empowering path that nurtures your life with rising prospects. It provides a transition to a journey that promotes balanced foundations and brings the room to grow your life in a unique direction.

8 Wednesday ~ Venus sextile Uranus 5:28

Spontaneity, fun, and fresh adventures rule your social life with this engaging sextile. It does crack the code to a brighter chapter. Something is on offer soon, which lands you in a wellspring of potential. You reveal new information about the path ahead. Sharing news and conversations with this person brings stable foundations that give you a feel for growing your social life. It opens the book on a new chapter in your world.

9 Thursday

Exploring diverse pathways will drive you towards prosperity if you feel stuck and restlessness comes calling. You can come up with creative solutions to age-old problems. Being open to developing your skills helps you unearth the kind of advancement that takes your talents to the next level. Know that you can work wonders to improve your situation.

10 Friday ~ Mercury conjunct Pluto 17:16

Today's conjunct between Mercury and Pluto offers intense curiosity to delve a little deeper into life's mysteries. Focusing on your inner terrain provides a healing and therapeutic quality which enables you to sweep away outworn areas. Dissolving sensitive areas and releasing the past helps nurture well-being. This inner work offers grounded foundations that help you achieve your best in life.

11 Saturday ~ Mercury ingress Aquarius 11:22

You can look forward to a refreshing change of pace. Prospects are heightening, bringing new terrain to explore. Indeed, several exciting avenues of growth light a path forward. It helps release the limitations that have blocked progress lately. It breaks up stagnant energy patterns and brings an energizing chapter to light. It brings a focus on social opportunities and gets a chance to mingle with your broader circle of friends.

12 Sunday

Advancing your life into unique areas takes you towards growth and rising prospects. Being adaptable and open to growing your life supports your dreams, allowing unique opportunities to crop up in your life. It leads to a richly creative and expressive environment that nurtures your well-being. It lets you channel excess energy into a journey imbued with potential and possibility. It connects you with kindred spirits who share similar values.

13 Monday ~ Last Quarter Moon in Scorpio 16:01

Life opens to a new flavor as an opportunity comes knocking. It creates space to develop your dreams and grow your world in a unique direction. Expanding the boundaries of your life draws transformation and happiness. It helps you get busy crafting your goals, and this lets you create concrete steps that offer tangible results. Advancement comes and provides a pleasing outcome.

14 Tuesday ~ Valentine's Day

A change of scene is on the horizon. Exploring options gets life on track as you reveal a pathway that offers transformation. It brings a compelling journey and a change of direction that opens the floodgates to a lively chapter. It brings lightness and harmony into your social life as an invitation to mingle crops up. It lets you achieve growth in heart matters—romance, magic, and companionship light a trailblazing path forward.

15 Wednesday ~ Venus conjunct Neptune 12:25

Venus joins forces with Neptune, and your love life takes on a dreamy quality as you engage in fanciful thoughts and contemplation. The desire moves into the realm of unlimited imagination as you think about the future, intending to nurture romance in your life. It draws active and thoughtful discussions and helps you promote a meaningful area.

16 Thursday ~ Saturn conjunct Sun 16:48

Saturn connects with the Sun to blaze a trail towards developing your goals. Getting serious about limiting distractions and cultivating discipline, concentration, and order will help you nail progress in your working life. Gaining traction on improving the security in your world will bring a valuable sense of achievement and accomplishment to your door.

17 Friday

You improve your life by being open to new possibilities. A new beginning is earmarked, which brings an active and enterprising chapter to light. It helps you get life on track to grow your goals. It opens the gates wide to new potential that shines a light on what you can achieve with the right approach. The path ahead glimmers brightly with refreshing potential. Being open to change facilitates growth.

18 Saturday ~ Mercury sextile Jupiter 2:13, Sun ingress Pisces 22:30

The Mercury Jupiter aspect creates harmony between both planets. It sparks rising curiosity, questioning, and fresh ideas. It helps you sweep away areas that are no longer relevant. Building grounded foundations in your life draw dividends. It sets in motion the essence of manifestation that gently shifts your focus towards developing goals you have in mind. It marks the beginning of a productive chapter that is a ticket for growth in your life.

19 Sunday ~ Venus sextile Pluto 17:04

Today's Venus and Pluto alignment offers depth and insight into your thought processes. It helps you dig a little deeper and discover what drives your passion. Thinking about the areas that hold the most significant meaning in your life can be helpful on many levels. It weeds out the areas that no longer are a good fit for your life by letting you see the most meaningful aspects of your world. Moving in alignment with the person you are becoming nurtures inspiration and passion.

20 Monday ~ Presidents' Day. New Moon in Pisces 7:08, Venus ingress Aries 7:52

Fundamental changes open the door wide to a new possibility. It brings a path that sees something impressive on offer. Planning lets you build your case and plot a trajectory that realizes a dream you have in mind. It does encourage you to move forward in alignment with an area that calls your name. You pour your energy into a venture that enriches and inspires you a great deal.

21 Tuesday ~ Shrove Tuesday (Mardi Gras), Mercury square Uranus 22:22

Original thinking, creative brainstorming, and insightful epiphanies are the order of the day as Mercury squares off against Uranus today. It brings creative projects and opportunities to work with your abilities. Several enticing options cross your path as new information opens a compelling route forward. It brings stable foundations that let you forge ahead towards enriching your life with new possibilities. Attractive options along bring a bounty of potential into your life.

22 Wednesday ~ Ash Wednesday, Lent Begins, Mercury trine Mars 20:14

A Mercury trine Mars aspect attracts a restless vibe. This cosmic alignment leaves you feeling spontaneous and ready for new adventures today. Life leads you to a time of pushing back boundaries as you embrace expanding horizons into new areas. You land in an encouraging environment that supports growth and progress. Paying attention to the unique options that cross your path draws valuable rewards.

23 Thursday

A transformation ahead brings lighter energy which offers a valuable boost to your spirit. It cultivates a beneficial path that connects you with implementing strategies that enable advancement. Focusing on steadily improving your life hits the sweet spot. It brings a journey of self-development that puts the spotlight on nurturing talents and refining your skills. A substantial endeavor emerges and illuminates a solid foundation from which to grow your life.

24 Friday

It is a time that brings new possibilities, which encourages you to expand your life and explore a social environment. It does see a person of interest coming forward; this is someone who resonates on your wavelength. It places you in the right place to nurture a bond of companionship. Open communication and social engagement paved the way forward for a new chapter in your social life.

25 Saturday

Your willingness to open the door to new possibilities draws a pleasing result for your social life. It offers a supportive landscape that nurtures well-being—an invitation to mingle cracks the code to a brighter chapter. Curious changes ahead bring a fresh cycle of growth into your life. Nurturing expansion connects to a magical time of sharing with kindred spirits. You land in an engaging environment that opens into a beautiful journey forward for your life.

26 Sunday

A social aspect ahead links you up with friends and companions. It draws a happy time of sharing ideas and engaging in thoughtful discussions. It brings fresh air into your surroundings that rejuvenate foundations from the ground up. Your social life gets a fortunate upgrade that brings the room to expand your circle of friends. It adds exciting spice and flavor to your life.

MARCH

Sun	Mon	Tue	Wed	Thu	Fri	Sat
			1	2	3	4
5	6	7	8	9	10	11
12	13	14	15	16	17	18
19	20	21	22	23	24	25
26	27	28	29	30	31	

NEW MOON

WORM MOON

27 Monday ~ First Quarter Moon in Gemini 8:06

Life lights up with new possibilities that encourage a shift forward. Focusing on freedom and expansion renews your soul and brings a unique approach into focus. It offers the perfect chance to develop goals that have been on the backburner. Setting intentions blends a mix of manifestations that helps crack the path wide open.

28 Tuesday

Refining your talents sharpens your abilities and shines a light on exciting possibilities. It brings a journey of discovery that is creative and inspiring. You reveal refreshing options that advance your skills as you peel back the layers. Keeping your eyes on the target enables you to aim correctly and achieve a bull's-eye for your vision. It gives you a leg up on an inspiring time that propels new options into your world.

1 Wednesday

A unique aspect supports learning and growth. Focusing your energy on a new interest does nurture your skills and talents. An opportunity appears soon, which positions you toward a chapter of prosperity. It brings a path that glimmers with options to explore. It does set the stage for an impressive time of advancing your vision. More freedom is ready to tempt you forward.

2 Thursday ~ Venus conjunct Jupiter 17:35, Mercury conjunct Saturn 14:34, Mercury ingress Pisces 22:49

Today's Venus conjunct Jupiter aspect is a positive sign for your social life. Expect an upward trend as rising prospects draw communication and invitations to mingle. It emphasizes a chapter of fresh beginnings, clarity, and insight that guide this process forward. It lets you dive into conversations that connect with your spirit in a happy environment.

3 Friday

You open a clear path that soothes your restless spirit. You begin a soul journey that lays the groundwork for a secure foundation. As you continue to build and stabilize your environment, you discover projects that let you use your gifts and abilities to powerful effect. Your circumstances are improving, and this draws balance and emotional well-being.

4 Saturday

Beautiful changes are coming into your life soon. There are going to be attractive possibilities that help you progress your vision. It brings a busy time that attracts support from other kindred spirits. Getting involved in a group environment adds fuel to your motivation, seeing your creativity skyrocket. It does bring a bountiful journey that charts an auspicious course forward.

5 Sunday

New potential triggers an open door that helps you remove blocks and limitations. Taking down the filters broadens your perception of what is possible when you set your mind to achieving a lofty goal. It brings a fruitful time that helps you move towards an energizing chapter. You burn away the anxiety and doubt and create a bridge towards your vision.

6 Monday ~ Purim (Begins at sundown), Sun sextile Uranus 13:41

This sextile heightens creativity and self-expression. You discover a new approach that boosts productivity and offers efficiency in your daily life. A new endeavor or project is likely to crop up, which takes you towards growth and prosperity. Examining your future goals allows you to strip away areas that are no longer relevant. Refinement distills the potential possible. It brews up a concoction that stirs the energy of manifestation.

7 Tuesday ~ Worm Full Moon in Virgo 12:40 Purim (Ends at sunset), Saturn ingress Pisces 13:03

A therapeutic pathway opens under the Full Moon and blossoms into a powerful journey forward for your life. It brings an extraordinary time that releases heaviness and extends your life to new possibilities. It helps you reawaken to the vibrant landscape of potential that surrounds your life. You discover an off-the-beaten-track journey that nurtures well-being and happiness.

8 Wednesday

Life brightens as you embark on growing the potential in your life. Clearing away the cobwebs lets you create a clean sweep that nurtures refreshing possibilities. Focusing on steadily improving your life hits the sweet spot as it cultivates a beneficial journey that connects you with rewarding outcomes. News arrives highlighting a little worn path that takes you towards a dream destination.

9 Thursday

A path of abundance opens that hits a high note. It brings a lovely time that motivates change. It has you focusing on an area that offers room to blossom into a stunning path forward. It brings feelings of abundance as it leads to nurturing a passion project that inspires your mind and heart. Something is brewing that brings a transition towards an exciting journey of self-discovery.

10 Friday

You achieve impressive results by your willingness to improve your life. The more you expand and grow your potential, the faster your talents blossom. You have gifts to share with others, focusing on developing your abilities transitioning your life to a new pathway that inspires your mind. It does let you test the waters in a new area. Doing research brings possibilities to light the way forward.

11 Saturday ~ Venus sextile Mars 15:04, Mercury sextile Uranus 21:04

Venus has your back today and draws social engagement into your life. There is a strong emphasis on fun and friendship ahead. It brings your social life to the forefront; surprises arrive to keep you guessing what's next. You build bonds that have room to grow ever stronger. It does set the scene for more abundant energy to flow into your world.

12 Sunday

A new option arrives, and you feel energized and excited about the potential. It does bring an opportunity by your willingness to look beneath the surface and dig deeper into new possibilities. Change is an essential theme that swirls around your life. This evolution is necessary; it can reinvent your aspect and bring a growth journey.

13 Monday

You turn a corner and head towards improving the foundations of your life. New energy lights up opportunities that offer improvement. It lets you advance your cause forward and extend your reach into new areas. It brings more balance into your surroundings, and you soon get settled in a productive and lively atmosphere. It generates plenty of leads that let you chart a path towards achievement and expansion.

14 Tuesday

Good news lands with a flurry of excitement. It enables you to expand your life and get busy developing a dynamic area that offers room to progress your goals. You will continue to spot opportunities and enjoy life by expanding your talents. Areas light up that offer growth and rising prospects. You soon get busy planning for future growth in this unique landscape filled with possibilities.

15 Wednesday ~ Last Q Moon in Sagittarius 2:08, Sun conjunct Neptune 23:39

You may feel sensitivities rising today as the Sun links up with Neptune in the sign of Pisces today. Intuition is sparking, and you can trust your gut instincts to guide you correctly when you reveal curious information that triggers your emotions. Listening to your gut instincts and intuition will help you spot the right path.

16 Thursday ~ Mercury conjunct Neptune 17:13, Sun square Mars 18:09,
Venus square Pluto 19:58, Venus ingress Taurus 22:31

Today, you may feel chaotic and under pressure as a great deal of cosmic energy disrupts stability in your life. Expect intensity as the Sun square Mars alignment may leave you feeling tense and hot under the collar. Creative expression and taking time to make yourself a priority will be beneficial in releasing frustrations and any heavy energy clinging to your spirit.

**17 Friday ~ St Patrick's Day. Mercury square Mars 4:48,
Sun conjunct Mercury 10:45, Venus sextile Saturn 20:25**

Today, Venus sextile Saturn promotes cooperation and offers the chance to join a joint project. It emphasizes expansion as an exciting vista tempts you forward. Embracing a life-affirming area brings well-being and grounded foundations into your life. It offers a chance to push back the barriers that limit progress as you get involved in expanding your situation.

18 Saturday

Life picks up speed and moves towards a faster pace, enabling you to make plans for future growth. You light a journey filled with hopes, dreams, and possibilities. Catching up with friends nurtures well-being and places you in the correct alignment to grow your social life. Opportunities ahead bring happiness into your world. You enter an exciting time that fosters warm expressions and heartfelt conversations.

19 Sunday ~ Mercury ingress Aries 4:22

Mercury transits into your first house of self, identity, and new beginnings. You enter a social time that shines brightly with light and active engagement. Sharing thoughts with valued companions leads to discussing a unique and vital assignment. This area is a pleasing showcase that enables you to take your talents to a broader audience. Rising confidence brings motivation and inspiration into your world. It offers room to share with friends.

20 Monday ~ Sun sextile Pluto 20:12, Sun ingress Aries 21:20, Ostara/Spring Equinox 21:25

Staying in tune with the influences that surround your life enables you to adjust course as needed to improve the prospects in your world. An area you channel your energy into developing soon returns a positive investment with an influx of inspiration. Working with your talents is a soothing balm that amplifies well-being. The journey brings an expansive chapter of rediscovery and rejuvenation.

21 Tuesday ~ New Moon in Pisces 17:22

Setting the bar higher brings a pleasing result. It helps you break past limitations and dive into an empowering phase of career growth. You build a bridge towards your vision by planning, preparing, and working towards your vision for future growth. Researching a unique area helps cultivate your talents and advance your skills. You stretch past your comfort zone and explore an exciting destination that calls your name.

22 Wednesday ~ Ramadan Begins

Information arrives soon that offers a lighter chapter. It brings a chance to dream about the possibilities as you crack the code to a brighter chapter. You head towards an active time of engaging with your social life. It brings outings and opportunities that feel spontaneous and adventurous. Keeping life vivid and dynamic draws happy times that uplift the mood. You find the right flavor by adding a dash of variety to your life.

23 Thursday ~ Pluto ingress Aquarius 8:42

An important decision cracks the code to improving your life. You pour your energy into an area that draws pleasing results. It connects with a social aspect that nurtures companionship. You discover a new role that brings well-being and harmony. It brings an end to delays as life moves forward, bringing an expansive and liberating phase that rekindles inspiration. It brings the motivation to expand the borders of your world.

24 Friday

A window of opportunity opens, and this helps you push stumbling blocks aside and rise to the occasion as you get busy and make the most of growing your life. It provides room to progress your talents into a new area. New possibilities tempt you towards an exciting landscape that is productive and innovative. Your willingness to explore various options helps you develop a winning trajectory.

25 Saturday ~ Mars ingress Cancer 11:36

Something extraordinary is about to appear in the road ahead for your life. It marks a time of happy surprises that bring a spontaneous element into your world. It ushers in a social aspect that feels enriching as it restores well-being and harmony to your spirit. Changes ahead beckon and tempt you towards expansion. It helps you break new ground.

26 Sunday

After some soul-searching, you will find a lighter vibration around your life. It helps you invest your time and energy in developing areas that hold the most significant meaning in your life. Reshaping goals revolutionizes the potential in your world. You gain a glimpse of glittering possibility and soon thrive in a busy and dynamic environment. Harnessing the power of your creativity cracks the code to advancing life forward.

27 Monday

You get a leg up to a new area that offers an assignment that grows your skills. Assessing the potential helps give you the green light to move forward and advance your abilities into a dynamic environment. Being open to new opportunities facilitates change that opens life to an exciting flavor. You achieve a handsome reward by being open to new possibilities. It brings the news that lights a promising path towards growth.

28 Tuesday ~ Mercury conjunct Jupiter 6:49

This astrological conjunct is perfect for brainstorming as ideas are big and expressive under this planetary influence. A business idea takes off and blossoms into growing your talents in a new area. Harnessing the magic within your creativity lets, you use the power of your skills to come up with viable options worth developing. You discover further leads that bring forward momentum into your life. It provides an avenue that advances your skills.

29 Wednesday ~ First Quarter Moon in Cancer 2:32

There will be important developments around your life soon; taking a closer look at the potential possible helps you unearth the right direction. You are ready for change, and a new chapter doesn't disappoint when it offers a trailblazing path forward. You hit your peak stride as you cultivate happiness and expansion in your social life.

30 Thursday ~ Mars trine Saturn 19:03, Venus conjunct Uranus 22:25

Mars forms a trine with Saturn today to give your working life wings. Hard work, dedication, and perseverance improve the day-to-day foundations of your life. Venus teams up with Uranus to add a dash of spontaneity to your social/personal life. As you set out on a new adventure, staying true to yourself will keep you aligned with the person you are becoming.

APRIL

Sun	Mon	Tue	Wed	Thu	Fri	Sat
						1
2	3	4	5	6	7	8
9	10	11	12	13	14	15
16	17	18	19	20	21	22
23	24	25	26	27	28	29
30						

New Moon

PINK MOON

31 Friday

Curious possibilities ramp up motivation and leave you feeling optimistic about the future. It brings a busy time that sees you concentrating on your goals. Developing your dreams promotes a productive and active time of progressing life forward. You make appropriate changes that enable things to get a significant shift along.

1 Saturday ~ All Fools/April Fool's Day

Setting intentions helps you work with the air of manifestation to bring good things your way. You are ready to discover new possibilities that reinvent many aspects of your life. Regularly reviewing progress helps you weed out areas best left behind as you forge ahead towards developing your dreams. You benefit from a busy and active time shared with friends.

2 Sunday ~ Palm Sunday.

Finding your groove and adopting a middle path forward nurtures greater security and grounded foundations. You discover you can achieve considerable advancement by growing your goals sustainably and moderately. Joining forces with friends and companions are creates a powerful synthesis that blends new ideas with fresh inspiration. Cultivating tranquillity helps you achieve remarkable outcomes.

3 Monday ~ Mercury ingress Taurus 16:20

Developing your plans keeps you feeling motivated and optimistic. A sweeter and more productive vibe is a positive influence that enables you to forge ahead and gain traction on developing your vision for future growth. Plans line up and open the way forward. It brings better security to your foundations, promoting balance and harmony in your life.

4 Tuesday

A curious assignment draws new responsibilities and a great outcome. It links you to a prosperous path that nurtures grounded foundations. New options ahead pull social engagement. It brings a busy time that offers a plethora of new opportunities. It connects you with a creative enterprise developed with other kindred spirits. Managing growth in a sustainable fashion enables you to tread lightly and build a progressive path forward for your life.

5 Wednesday ~ Passover (begins at sunset), Mercury sextile Saturn 16:18

With Mercury in sextile with Saturn, communication skills are rising. Enhanced clarity and mental insight help you understand more significant concepts, thought processes, and ideas with ease today. This cosmic enhancement enables you to step beyond traditional or repetitive learning and take your studies/working life to the next level. It helps you rise to the challenge and pole vault successfully over the hump day.

6 Thursday ~ Lent Ends. Pink Full Moon in Libra 4:37

It is a time that can see a heightening of sensitive emotions. Making yourself a priority draws well-being. It lights a path that nurtures your life on many levels. It brings an increase of hope, happiness, and optimism that is sure to buoy your spirits. An enticing aspect is stirring in the background that will come full when the right opportunity is ready to appear in your life.

7 Friday ~ Good Friday, Venus sextile Neptune 17: 59

Today's planetary alignment offers a mindful, spiritual aspect that is in keeping with the spirit of Easter. Venus sends loving beams into your home and family life, harmonizing bonds and drawing the essence of rejuvenation and renewal. Difficulties fade away as you rekindle inspiration. A fantastic outlook ahead attracts optimism and joy.

8 Saturday ~ Mercury sextile Mars 6:23

A sextile between Mercury and Mars sharpens cognitive abilities today. Mental clarity is on the rise, giving you valuable insight into the path ahead. Something you have been dearly hoping for reaches fruition. Positive signs ahead give you a glimmer of insight into the way forward. You enter a transformational aspect that renews the potential possible in your world. It brings a beautiful journey that takes your breath away as it promotes great happiness in your world.

9 Sunday ~Easter Sunday

You are moving away from a problematic aspect that has limited progress. You soon see victory looming overhead as you get the ball rolling on expanding your life. It brings unexpected developments in your social life that bring great joy into your world. Connecting with your cohorts brings new ideas and inspiration to contemplate.

10 Monday

Good news ahead brings a significant shift forward that teams you up with rising prospects. It offers an uptick of new options that have you feeling energized and ready to tackle new projects with a view towards advancement. You discover a unique opportunity that captures the essence of inspiration and enables you to build grounded foundations that offer room to improve home life. It brings inspiration and heightened security.

11 Tuesday ~ Venus ingress Gemini 4:43, Venus trine Pluto 10:14, Sun Conjunct Jupiter 22:07, Mercury at Greatest Elong 19.5E

Significant change brings a chapter that empowers and enriches your life. Being proactive draws a pleasing result as swift improvements follow the expansion of horizons around your life. You ramp up the potential possible by being flexible and adaptive to change. Communication arrives that shines the light around deepening friendships. An opportunity for collaboration offers growth and a sense of kinship.

12 Wednesday

An option arrives that helps you push back the barriers and expand your horizons into a new area. It marks a freedom-driven time that captures the essence of creativity. A lighter, more vibrant environment ahead opens the floodgates to an enterprising time of growth. Getting the chance to branch your talents out and develop new areas brings excitement into your world.

13 Thursday ~ Passover (ends at sunset), Last Quarter Moon in Capricorn 9:11

A surge of optimism opens the window to a brighter chapter. It illuminates a lighter environment that helps you craft a journey towards an inspiring goal. You discover plenty to celebrate as you set off in a new direction. Releasing the outworn energy dissolves sensitive areas. It creates space for a new life cycle that draws refreshing options. Putting the shine on your talents takes your abilities to the next level.

14 Friday ~ Orthodox Good Friday, Venus square Saturn 16:38

A Venus square Saturn encourages taking personal inventory of meaningful areas in your life. Adjusting course as necessary will give private bonds the best chance of success. Shining a more intensive light on interpersonal situations in your social life helps you see the truth and cut away from outworn areas. Set firm boundaries if a drama llama is in your circle of friends.

15 Saturday

New foundations emerge in your life that wipes the slate clean. Being proactive about seeking out opportunities draws a pleasing result for your life. It connects you with an upbeat time that sees life moving faster. Meeting new people brings a fresh start that offers a rosy time for developing interpersonal bonds.

16 Sunday ~ Orthodox Easter

Making yourself a priority puts your needs and desires front and center. It allows you to expand your life and connect with a companion who nurtures a wellspring of potential in your social life. It has you exploring a journey that feels right for your soul. Rejuvenation and renewal bring a clean slate of potential into your life.

17 Monday

Being clear about things helps you cut away from toxic influences that limit you from reaching your highest trajectory. Not everyone is deserving of your time and attention. Being discerning helps trim the deadwood holding you back; successes add up as you begin a phase that promotes greater security and balance in your life.

18 Tuesday

Information arrives that illustrates refreshing potential around your life. A new array of options has you thinking about developing a side journey. It brings an outstanding chapter where you achieve significant outcomes by being open to new possibilities. It draws a time of movement and discovery that lets you take in new horizons. Exciting changes ahead bring a remarkable trajectory of progression and growth.

19 Wednesday

Tapping into your wildest instincts helps you carve out a journey that speaks to your soul. It liberates the areas of creativity, passion, and inspiration. A far-flung destination comes into view, and you soon become busy building a bridge towards a brighter future. Achieving your goals ignites progression as life heads to an exciting upswing.

20 Thursday ~ Ramadan Ends, New Moon in Taurus 4:12, Hybrid Solar Eclipse, Sun ingress Taurus 8:09, Sun square Pluto 16:26

The Sun square Pluto aspect draws renewal and rejuvenation. Pluto charts a course towards transformation and offers a highly creative part that lights the way forward towards improving your circumstances. The Sun contributes golden beings that offer harmony, transcendence, and rising prospects. This planetary combo elevates creative inclinations due to a New Moon.

21 Friday ~ Mercury turns Retrograde in Taurus at 8:34

Mercury plays havoc with interpersonal bonds and can send communication haywire during its retrograde phase. Buckle up; it's going to be a bumpy ride as your social life goes on a Mercury-driven rollercoaster. If someone's communication triggers an emotional aspect, be mindful that this planetary phase is best with a balanced and understanding approach. Focusing on staying flexible will give you a solid basis as you navigate forward.

22 Saturday ~ Earth Day, Lyrids Meteor Shower from April 16th -25th

You receive news that offers a social opportunity. Mingling and networking see life bubbling along and heading towards smoother sailing. The rhythm and pace propel you forward towards new possibilities. It lets you reap the rewards of expansion around your social life as a new companion emerges. Expanding your circle of friends shines a light on building stable foundations.

23 Sunday

Life expands outwardly, which clears the way towards an active and happy chapter of networking with friends. You invest time and energy in developing an area that enriches your life. It brings a time of chasing dreams and setting goals. Improvement in your home territory becomes a strong focus. You strike gold by expanding your circle of friends as it lets you turn a corner and head into a winning chapter of nurturing companionship.

24 Monday ~ Mercury sextile Mars 3:22

Quick reflexes enable you to spot the diamond in the rough. The Mercury sextile with Mars offers new leads. Life gets a boost as you open a pathway that leads to growth. Beautiful changes ahead support your vision to elevate and advance life forward. Things fall into place with a sense of synchronicity as you move towards a busy and exciting time. Good news arrives with a flurry of lighter energy; it brings the wind beneath your wings, as it inspires you on many levels.

25 Tuesday ~ Sun sextile Saturn 10:47

Today's sextile brings opportunities that light a path forward. It illuminates fantastic potential that enables you to improve your circumstances. Exploring leads creates new possibilities that draw a productive time of developing your working life in a new area. A new role on offer brings a rapid change that illustrates the potential ready to bloom in your life. News and information carry you towards a site that offers growth and prosperity.

26 Wednesday

Essential news arrives that points the way forward. It connects you with a positive aspect that draws opportunities to mingle with people. It lays the foundations for improvement in your life. It draws a light-hearted time of social engagement that marks a turning point. Expanding your life encourages balance as it fortifies your world with enriching experiences.

27 Thursday ~ First Quarter Moon in Leo 21:20

A meticulous approach to improving your circumstances brings opportunities that create a bridge to a brighter chapter. It emphasizes self-expression, identity, and creativity. It brings an efficient and productive time that brings you closer to your goals. Growing your skills and refining your talents has a powerful effect on improving the foundations in your life. It sparks a path that advances towards an engaging time.

28 Friday

Building more stability in your life helps ease the stress and nurture a fresh start in your world. It ushers in forward momentum that draws a better balance between your career goals and personal life. Finding the proper sense of balance and equilibrium in your world promotes higher potential in your romantic life. It draws warmth and abundance as you plot a course towards rising prospects in your social life.

29 Saturday ~ Mars sextile Uranus 8:04

This sextile brings unique ideas that help you think outside the box to obtain innovative solutions. Uranus places the focus on rebellion, liberation, freedom. It adds a dash of spontaneity into your life that marks a time of social expansion. Life offers new possibilities to tempt you forward. It gives you the green light to step boldly forward and embrace a more connected and social environment.

30 Sunday

Lively discussions give you the green light to get the ball rolling on developing your social life. It sets the tone for an exciting time shared with friends and companions. Life becomes more active and engaging, opening the way towards rising prospects. It brings a peak time for creativity as new ideas help you craft a blossoming path forward for your life.

MAY

Sun	Mon	Tue	Wed	Thu	Fri	Sat
	1	2	3	4	5	6
7	8	9	10	11	12	13
14	15	16	17	18	19	20
21	22	23	24	25	26	27
28	29	30	31			

AQUARIUS

VIRGO TAURUS

SCORPIO MARS STARS SUN

WEDDING WEALTH FORTUNE

ARIES CAPRICORN CALENDAR

LOVE ASTROLOGY MONTH

GEMINI MOON

HOROSCOPE

LEO

SAGITTARIUS HAPPINESS

BIRTHDAY ASTRONOMY

CANCER LIBRA NEPTUNE DATE ZODIAC

EARTH SIGN

PISCES SKY

TODAY DAILY WEEKLY

CONSTELLATION MONTHLY

NEW MOON

FLOWER MOON

1 Monday ~ Beltane/May Day, Pluto turns retrograde in Aquarius 18:39, Sun conjunct Mercury 23:27

Pluto is the modern ruler of Scorpio; it symbolizes how we experience power, renewal, rebirth, and mysterious or subconscious forces. This retrograde phase lasts until October. It allows you to dive deep and explore inner realms and darker aspects of your personality ordinarily hidden from view. Understanding your psyche on a deeper level provides access to the forces driving your personality. It lets you comprehend the why and wherefore's behind desires.

2 Tuesday

A more stable landscape emerges soon. It does bring a welcome shift forward that increases the potential possible. Life expands at a comfortable pace as you draw profitable opportunities that focus on improving your circumstances. It does let you embrace life-affirming endeavors that stabilize and bring balance into your environment. Friends tempt you out into the broader community.

3 Wednesday

Your creativity is increasing; this stirs the pot of potential and tempts you towards developing your skills further. It leads to a rich and expressive environment that allows you to harness your energy into areas that offer growth and abundance. If you have been struggling with uncertainty, this resolves as the path ahead clears and beckons you into new territory.

4 Thursday ~ Venus square Neptune 17:40

A Venus square Neptune aspect offers a dreamy quality. It provides the perfect vibe for engaging in the big sky dreaming about your perfect romantic escapade. While fairytales in the sky offer relaxation and escapism, it's important to remember that this dreaminess could lead to delusion if you overly focus on something currently out of reach. Understanding the escapism and creative elements at play enables you to dream big and still feel grounded in reality.

5 Friday ~ Venus sextile Jupiter 4:02, Flower Full Moon in Scorpio 17:34 Penumbral Lunar Eclipse

Venus and Jupiter's sextile create beneficial and harmonious vibrations for your romantic life. Good luck and rising prospects bring warmth and social engagement. Necessary changes occur that attract the right people into your life. It does get a social time that allows you to gain traction on your vision. It paves the way forward towards a lively and productive inspirational chapter.

6 Saturday ~ Eta Aquarids Meteor Shower April 19th - May 28th

You benefit from developments on the horizon. It brings blessings as you head towards a productive chapter that is lively and dynamic. It's a busy time that helps you build solid foundations that nurture a stable phase of growth and prosperity. It leaves you feeling optimistic about the future. New inspiration sweeps into your life that clears the path forward.

7 Sunday ~ Venus ingress Cancer 14:20

Information ahead enables you to progress your vision. It connects you with a more abundant chapter. Releasing blocks creates space to nurture your creativity. It does draw new possibilities into your life. It brings the essence of manifestation. It sees you settle gently into a new chapter that offers abundance. It does get a social environment that adds glamour to your life.

8 Monday

Life supports your efforts to improve circumstances. New possibilities spark a journey that offers expansion. It shines a light on goals, status, and career success. Putting the finishing touches on your strategy lets you develop a winning trajectory when news arrives that encourages expansion. Rising prospects open up an avenue that offers growth and security. It allows you to move towards advancement.

9 Tuesday ~ Sun conjunct Uranus 19:55

A vital shift forward brings expansion. It does link you up with a new chapter that enables you to circulate in your broader community. Necessary changes occur that attract the right people into your life. It does bring a social time that allows you to gain traction on your vision. It paves the way forward towards a lively and productive inspirational chapter. It brings a time of magic and abundance.

10 Wednesday

A great deal of potential comes that takes you towards a phase of expansion, prosperity, and growth. It has you working on larger goals. It brings a venture that captures your interest. This area gives you a chance to develop an endeavor that inspires your mind. It is a good time when you take steps towards progressing your goals. There is plenty to celebrate ahead; a gathering of friends brings lively discussions.

11 Thursday

News arrives that brings change. A focus on your home environment gives you the chance to build a robust foundation to expand life outwardly. The wheels are in motion, bringing a lively and engaging landscape into focus. Surprise communication opens the path ahead towards developing a unique endeavor. It ushers in a time of lively discussions that restore balance. It links you up with a project that is the right fit for your restlessness.

12 Friday ~ Mercury sextile Saturn 8:32, Last Quarter Moon in Aquarius 14:28

Mercury sextile Saturn gives your Friday a boost which helps you tidy up loose ends before the weekend. Mental acuity rises, bringing a focused mind and increased powers of observation lets you see what needs addressing. Today's other cognitive improvements include excellent concentration, good memory, and organization skills. With everything running smoothly in your working life, you can enjoy the weekend ahead knowing you have taken care of business.

13 Saturday ~ Mercury sextile Venus 2:41, Venus trine Saturn 6:56

Mercury sextile Venus offers a social and friendly influence making this a great day to connect with your tribe. It does draw significant time where you can improve your circumstances. This aspect brings a gateway forward that opens a path of plenty. It brings an enchanting chapter where you harness the magic within your spirit to stellar effect.

14 Sunday ~ Mother's Day (US)

It speaks of new possibilities arriving that pave the way for a solid foundation. It does improve the stability and equilibrium possible in your situation. Your dedication and perseverance win out. It takes you towards developing goals and embracing the rewards of your work. There is a spotlight on home and family, reaping abundance, and appreciating all the blessings in your world.

15 Monday ~ Mercury turns direct in Taurus 3:16, Mars trine Neptune 13:44

With Mercury turning direct today, the focus is on your social life. Mars forms a trine with Neptune, enhancing potential as confidence rises and you feel ready for social engagement. It offers the perfect solution for the dodgems as you get busy being self-expressive, communicative, and creative.

16 Tuesday ~ Jupiter ingress Taurus 17:01

A curious assignment comes calling and lights up pathways that offer growth, learning, and self-development. Being open to unique possibilities washes away outworn areas that are no longer relevant to your current goals. You discover you can navigate an ever-changing pathway with flexibility and adaptability.

17 Wednesday

A breakthrough ahead rains unique potential in your life. It creates space to focus on developing your skills. As you shake off the heavy vibrations that have dialed in your creativity, you release the past. You discover you can truly thrive in a unique and dynamic landscape. New options become a catalyst for growth. An original and innovative journey forward rules the way of advancement in your working life as you take in a new area of learning.

18 Thursday ~ Jupiter square Pluto 1:09, Sun sextile Neptune 8:59

Today's Jupiter square Pluto brings extra drive and increased energy to complete projects and finish up your to-do list. Neptune also boosts your goals as a sextile with the Sun helps you find the resources and support needed to manifest your vision. You can bring your dreams to reality as the planets have your back today, attracting rising prospects into your life.

19 Friday ~ Mercury sextile Saturn 6:50 New Moon in Taurus 15:54

Today, Mercury, Saturn sextile boosts your communication skills and confidence. Add in a dash of New Moon inspiration and aspiration, and you have the perfect mix for engaging in brainstorming with valued companions. Sharing ideas and adding creative ingredients into the pot of manifestation helps you develop a winning trajectory from which to grow your world next month.

20 Saturday ~ Mars ingress Leo 15:24

Mars lands in Leo, and this raises confidence. It's time to go big and be proud and bold. You benefit from developments on the horizon. It brings blessings as you head towards a productive chapter that is lively and dynamic. It's a busy time that helps you build solid foundations that nurture a stable phase of growth and prosperity. It leaves you feeling optimistic about the future. New inspiration sweeps into your life that clears the path forward.

21 Sunday ~ Mars opposed Pluto 3:11, Sun ingress Gemini 7:04,
Sun trine Pluto 13:58

Mars connects with a competitive edge today that could see your authority tested. The Sun trine Pluto aspect also adds fuel to the fire as it increases your desire to gain power and feed your ambitious streak. You seek opportunities to elevate your standing among peers and co-workers today. Climbing the ladder towards success becomes a dominant factor.

22 Monday ~ Victoria Day (Canada), Sun sextile Mars 5:56

The Sun sextile Mars transit brings vital energy and renewed zest for life. Your creativity is increasing; this stirs the pot of potential and tempts you towards developing your skills further. It leads to a rich and expressive environment that allows you to harness your energy into areas that offer growth and abundance. If you have been struggling with uncertainty, this resolves as the path ahead clears and beckons you into new territory.

23 Tuesday ~ Mars square Jupiter 5:13

Today's Mars square Jupiter offers a positive influence that increases stamina and boosts your energy. Enthusiasm for the task at hand rises, boosting productivity and enabling you to deal with the day's demands efficiently and capably. It provides new options that open a gateway towards growth. Being receptive to change lets you flex your talents and take in new areas which offer rising prospects. A pioneering attitude blazes a path towards new adventures.

24 Wednesday

As you create a bridge towards growing your dreams, you discover a venture that opens the door wide. A turning point occurs that offers advancement for your working life. It lets you dive into uncharted territory and find growth is possible when you push against the barriers of perceived expectations. An opportunity ahead fosters rising optimism. You get involved in learning an area that holds water and revs up the success rate for your career.

25 Thursday ~ Shavuot (Begins at sunset)

You face a crossroads, and a decision is required to step past this juncture and head towards your vision. There is a path that speaks to your heart directly. Your intuition guides this process, and you feel it is the right direction to go down. It does see you heading towards change, as you reveal hidden depths of insight that enable progress to occur. Removing the confusion allows for a unique journey to blossom.

26 Friday ~ Venus sextile Uranus 7:36

Today's sextile promotes a vibrant and active social life. With Venus charming and Uranus adding a dash of spontaneity to your weekend plans, it assures a fun and lively time shared with friends. You travel a journey that dazzles with exciting options, leading to a unique phase of growing dreams. As you move forward, you connect with exceptional people and curious opportunities that continue to grow your life outwardly.

27 Saturday ~ Shavuot (Ends at sunset), First Quarter Moon in Virgo 15:22

Exciting news ahead brings a solid focus on your social circle. It propels you towards a journey of promise and progression. Sweeping changes on the horizon bring a time of socializing that cultivates companionship. Being open to meeting new people shapes the path ahead into a journey worth growing. It places you in the proper alignment to network with friends and draws companionship into your world.

28 Sunday

Making yourself a priority is a gateway to growing your dreams. It brings a busy time that focuses on improving the security in your life. Evaluating the path ahead and moving away from areas that failed to reach fruition is vital in achieving gold. Creativity and inspiration burn brightly over the coming weeks, advancing life to new endeavors.

JUNE

Sun	Mon	Tue	Wed	Thu	Fri	Sat
				1	2	3
4	5	6	7	8	9	10
11	12	13	14	15	16	17
18	19	20	21	22	23	24
25	26	27	28	29	30	

NEW MOON

STRAWBERRY MOON

29 Monday ~ Memorial Day, Mercury at Greatest Elongation 24.9W

You spend time in a supportive and nurturing environment. Events align to nourish your soul and expand the borders of your world. It illustrates a time of lively discussions that offer an open road of potential in your life. There will be a chance to plan a trip away, something to work on to bring a goal into focus.

30 Tuesday

Stirring the pot of manifestation brings impressive results to your door. Being available to change brings a time of growth and prosperity that restores equilibrium and gives a more stable basis to the foundations in your life. Your willingness to be open to developing your world creates remarkable progress. New ideas and options arrive to tempt you forward.

31 Wednesday

Changes ahead nurture a growth-orientated environment. It brings a landmark time to head towards growth and success. Plotting your goals keeps you one step forward from the rest. It lets you build a life in a productive, efficient, and expansive fashion. It brings refreshing options that nurture your abilities and grow your talents.

1 Thursday

Life brings an opportunity you can embrace. A new source of prosperity arrives, letting you create progress. It does see you resolving a problematic aspect and swimming upstream; you soon discover smoother waters that draw stability. It brings a magic possibility that lights the path forward. It is a fantastic time to initiate new projects; reviewing your strategy enables you to tweak the potential and obtain strong growth.

2 Friday ~ Venus trine Neptune 22:42

Creativity and imagination are peaking under the blissful Venus, Neptune trine. Harmony, equilibrium, and well-being soar under this positive influence. Self-expression is rising, cultivating a unique path that captures the essence of artistic inclinations. Venus showers positivity over your social life, improving personal bonds.

3 Saturday

Today speaks of security and abundance on the home front. It does bring a time of new goals that let you build on the foundations you have already created. It does bring growth, and you make fantastic progress on developing your vision. It sees a shift forward that turns the leaf on a new chapter and brings abundance into focus. It does get an enterprising section that fits perfectly with your lifestyle.

**4 Sunday ~ Strawberry Full Moon in Sagittarius 3:42,
Mercury conjunct Uranus 19:50**

Mercury and Uranus form a positive aspect that heightens mental abilities. Increasing mental stimulation promotes fresh ideas in your life today. Technology and communication play a part in fostering possibilities for future development. Curiosity leads to an uplifting time discussing future projects and endeavors with a kindred spirit who understands your outlook on life.

5 Monday ~ Venus ingress Leo 13:42, Venus opposed Pluto 16:04

Researching options and planning a strategy raises confidence. It helps you move forward with courage and conviction towards developing your vision for future growth. You soon get the feeling that everything is clicking into place as you reveal a unique option that feels tailor-made for your life. You trigger a journey of expanding opportunities by being flexible and open to change.

6 Tuesday

New options ahead offer an environment ripe for growth. Doing research and exploring leads helps you connect with people who can assist and offer advice. The tides turn in your favor as a positive influence emerges that brings exciting prospects to the surface. It brings expansion that enables you to fill depleted emotional tanks with engaging conversations and a heightened sense of well-being. It lays the foundations for a stable and balanced journey.

7 Wednesday

You emerge from a quiet time you have been resting in recently. It does bring a time of celebration; you embrace a dynamic and exciting chapter. It does see an opportunity opening, which lets you join forces with another to develop a long-term goal. It brings a serious commitment to developing your vision. It is a good time to progress your goals.

8 Thursday

A new approach to life helps you harness a fresh start and begin a chapter that resonates warmly with your spirit. An artistic flair has you thinking big about possibilities. You may decide to backtrack and rediscover an old project that has been on the backburner. An entrepreneurial role or innovative approach draws dividends. It may see a business idea take off, which begins a journey towards uncharted territory.

9 Friday

Information ahead lets you gain insight into an area of interest. It does bring a time of inspired possibilities that puts you in an optimistic mood. You discover a social environment that takes you towards an active time of personal growth. It does see you tap into a path that offers room to grow and evolve. This information helps you find the situation that hits the right note in your life.

10 Saturday ~ Last Quarter Moon in Pisces 19:31

There are opportunities to head out into a more social environment soon. It does bring the time of communication when a message arrives that tempts you out into your broader community. It is a fantastic chapter where you nurture your soul and draw rejuvenation into your life. Spending time with kindred spirits lays the groundwork for an active and productive environment.

11 Sunday ~ Mercury ingress Gemini 10:24, Mercury trine Pluto 10:27, Pluto ingress Capricorn 13:12, Venus square Jupiter 15:39

Today's Venus square Jupiter planetary alignment offers good things for your social life. It is the perfect time to engage with friends; lively discussions nurture creativity. It is a prime time for letting your hair down and having fun in a relaxing environment that draws stability into your world.

12 Monday

You draw new possibilities into your life. It does heighten the potential possible and let you develop an area of interest. It connects you with others who resonate on the same wavelength. Taking time to share your creative ideas with them does bring a potent brew of potential into your life. It brings you to an extensive chapter where you can manifest positive outcomes by exploring innovative pathways towards growth.

13 Tuesday

You are currently transitioning to a new phase. It brings news that inspires; it shines a spotlight on new options. Information makes a dashing entrance, carrying a theme of improving your circumstances that resonates beautifully with your spirit. Your pioneering abilities are put to good use with a creative undertaking soon.

14 Wednesday ~ Flag Day

You scale new heights and reach for a lofty goal. It brings a time of working with your skills and evolving your talents as you take on a learning course and cultivate more significant opportunities for your life. A new financial or career option appears and brings rising prospects into your life. It brings a journey of new beginnings, opportunities, and potential.

15 Thursday

The changes ahead keep you on your feet. It does bring the pep into your life when a burst of new energy makes a dashing appearance. You get busy working with a path that offers room for progression. There is plenty to do, and this brings a productive chapter that provides a bountiful time. It sets you off on a prosperous cycle and activates your creativity to a stellar effect. You can amplify the results possible by staying open and flexible. Adaptability is essential.

16 Friday

You find your circle of friends expands as you experience a new beginning on many levels. It brings change, friendship, and companionship into your world. It is a time of expansion that connects you with unique people and grows your life outwardly. An enriching time that flows into your social life soon. It does bring invitations to circulate with friends and kindred spirits. Being with your crew is therapeutic; it draws balance into your world.

17 Saturday ~ Saturn turns Retrograde in Pisces 16:52

Saturn is a planet that rules boundaries, structure, and discipline. This retrograde draws balance and righteousness into your situation. Making fair and reasonable choices and decisions connects with karma to achieve a fair and beneficial outcome. You may be about to face a decision in your life. Facing the truth of a situation shines a light on where the scales may be tipped unevenly to one side, creating a sense of imbalance in your life.

18 Sunday ~ New Moon in Cancer 4:38, Father's Day (US)

Your river of hopes and dreams merge with a sea of understanding about the path ahead. It brings goals that make your life a priority. It focuses on developing your world in alignment with the person you are currently becoming. Life becomes a blaze of activity and opportunity. The power of magic stimulates creative growth and lets you manifest rewarding outcomes.

19 Monday ~ Sun square Neptune 3:53, Jupiter sextile Saturn 15:53

Today, the Neptune square Sun aspect can water down your ambitions, leaving you feeling foggy and indecisive. If your vision feels clouded, going back over your plans can help make sure they continue to align with your vision for future growth. Recommitting to developing your career goals can help shift some of the clouds that hang over your working life today. If the boss gives you a hard time, blame it on Neptune for bringing Monday woes into your working life.

20 Tuesday

Growing opportunities is a defining moment that cracks the code to a brighter chapter. Through careful planning and concentrated effort, you achieve a pleasing result for your life. It brings a path of pure potentiality into your life. This abundant chapter is a journey that can be grown and developed.

21 Wednesday ~ Midsummer/Litha Solstice 14:58, Mercury sextile Mars 15:23

The Mercury sextile Mars aspect today fosters joint projects and cooperation. Getting involved with a group endeavor stimulates your mind and brings new possibilities. Brainstorming sessions offer a trailblazing path towards innovative solutions and rising prospects. Joining forces and strategizing with like-minded people cultivate an excellent success rate. It helps you cover the bases by blending other people's talents into the mix of potential at your disposal.

22 Thursday

There is such abundance swirling around the periphery of your life. It does see a positive factor flow into your world that resonates with vibrant conversations. It activates a time of personal growth. As you move in alignment with your heart, your willingness to open to new possibilities is instrumental in creating positive change. It does bring an option that is perfect for development.

23 Friday

A restlessness within your spirit sends vibrations to expand horizons and draw something new into your life. It does activate a fascinating chapter that brings new possibilities to explore. You may see your path diverging from your current trajectory. It draws a more spiritual and focused alignment that is in harmony with the person you are currently becoming.

24 Saturday

A fork in the road ahead does bring a decision; it creates an essential change that lets you take a journey towards achieving a goal that is dear to your heart. Under challenging conditions, you have had to come up with new solutions. It does help you launch towards a vision that holds promise. Luck and good fortune are with you and support this expansion. It does let you enter a chapter imbued with growth potential.

25 Sunday

The path ahead illuminates a creative undertaking. It does have you thinking about developing your visionary ideas and starting to grow your skills. A design you hatch over the coming weeks soon takes on a life of its own. It does help you stay busy and active. It draws a time of lively discussions and stimulating conversations with other kindred spirits.

26 Monday ~ First Quarter Moon in Libra 7:50, Mars square Uranus 9:22

Being mindful of goals and dreams helps create a journey towards your vision. It brings a sense of purpose and added momentum into your life. It lets you move forward with courage and conviction as you open a new chapter in your book of life. It has you feeling optimistic about the potential possible in your world.

27 Tuesday ~ Mercury ingress Cancer 12:22

The events ahead set in motion remarkable opportunities for growth. Curious changes along bring an improvement of circumstances into your life. It shines a light on advancing your situation forward as new information reveals a side journey that shimmers with possibility. It connects you with others who radiate your frequency; it brings a group activity that nurtures lively discussions and well-being.

28 Wednesday

Curious changes ahead bring improvement into your world. It rebalances energy as it draws stability into your home life. It creates foundations that offer room to build balance; you enjoy a calming and settled environment that creates space for developing new projects and endeavors. It helps you create the kind of change you seek as it offers excitement around a burgeoning creative enterprise. Acting on instincts draws impressive results.

29 Thursday ~ Sun trine Saturn 1:42

Today's Sun trine Saturn offers constructive dialogues and thoughtful ideas that enhance your creativity and stimulate new pathways of possibility in your life. A positive influence nurtures unique approaches that capitalize on the potential possible in your surroundings. You uncover information that promotes curious new developments in your life. It sets the stage to cultivate a journey towards greener pastures. It connects you with your circle of friends.

JULY

Sun	Mon	Tue	Wed	Thu	Fri	Sat
						1
2	3	4	5	6	7	8
9	10	11	12	13	14	15
16	17	18	19	20	21	22
23	24	25	26	27	28	29
30	31					

ARIES

NEW MOON

BUCK MOON

30 Friday ~ Neptune turns Retrograde in Pisces, 19:28

Neptune retrograde strips away delusions, allusions, and fanciful thinking. Under the glare of more informed thought processes, you build tangible growth pathways to take your talents to the next level. This phase enables you to sink your teeth in developing goals that offer fruitful results. Moving away from areas that have clouded your thinking and brought doubt to your judgment does provide you with clear stepping stones that take you towards success.

1 Saturday ~ Canada Day, Sun conjunct Mercury 5:05, Mercury sextile Jupiter 7:10, Sun sextile Jupiter 10:26

Open-mindedness, curiosity, and a quest for adventure are prominent aspects as a Mercury sextile Jupiter alignment fosters creativity and self-expression. This transit favors organization, planning, and the development of longer-term goals. Reviewing plans and streamlining your vision enables you to cut to the chase and find a practical path to progress your goals. New information emerges to catch your interest and spur you to advance your life.

2 Sunday ~ Venus square Uranus 14:32

An increased need for freedom and liberation can destabilize as Venus faces Uranus in a square alignment. Being mindful of balancing interpersonal bonds while being self-expressive and creative can ease tensions. At the same time, you can let your hair down and enjoy a freedom-driven chapter of fun and excitement.

3 Monday ~ Super Moon, Buck Full Moon in Capricorn 11:40

Communication arrives that shines the light around friendships and collaboration. It offers growth and kinship with friends and companions. It is a refreshing change as you sweep the drama in your social life out to sea, and you set sail toward smoother waters. Today's Full Moon brings healing and abundance; it fires up the areas of self-expression, confidence, and creativity.

4 Tuesday ~ Independence Day

Staying open to new opportunities brings a busy season of social engagement. It transports healing energy to your mind, body, and spirit. It is a time of celebration and harmony that draws your nearest and dearest close. Lively discussions and thoughtful dialogues usher in a chapter of happiness. Opportunities arise out of the blue that sparks your interest, which can see a leap into the unknown.

5 Wednesday

A breakthrough occurs regarding a dream that previously seemed out of reach. It hits the ticket for a productive time of developing life in a new direction. Projects crop up that inspire you and encourage the innovative use of your skills. Investigating options brings a cycle of growth that expands horizons. It ushers in a trailblazing path forward for your life.

6 Thursday

Challenges are invitations to growth and self-development. A new venture brings a flurry of inspiration into your world. It lets you harness creative abilities and focus on developing your gifts to a new level. Advancing your potential forward takes you to a prosperous landscape. It enables you to gain traction on your long-term goals.

7 Friday

Opportunities to mingle ahead encourage constructive dialogues that bring a new perspective into your life. It draws a fruitful time of positive influences that bring new options to your table. The way forward becomes bright and optimistic as you get the chance to rebrand your image in an exciting new area.

8 Saturday

News arrives that kicks off a chapter of improving your life. It triggers an active phase of developing new goals and getting involved in the broader world of potential outside of your front door. You create a grounded and stable environment from which to grow your dreams. It brings a time of connecting with friends and mingling with people who inspire growth and progress in your world.

9 Sunday ~ Mercury trine Neptune 23:56

Mercury in trine with Neptune focuses on your dreams and goals; it adds mental clarity that helps you stay focused as you work towards realizing your vision. Something you hope to reach in your life can reach fruition with the correct planning, adjustments, and focus. Creating space to nurture your priorities lets you reap the rewards of a dedicated approach that offers an increasing success rate.

10 Monday ~ Last Quarter Moon in Aries 1:48, Mars ingress Virgo 11:34, Mercury opposed Pluto 20:47

You receive news that brings a boost into your world. It has a powerful effect as it provides a new landscape of options. It draws a happy shift forward that lets you release areas that have caused blocks and lack of progress. Refining and streamlining your situation amplifies potential and enables you to turn a corner and head towards growth.

11 Tuesday ~ Mercury ingress Leo 4:09

This transit speaks of lovely changes that arrive soon. It does let you land in the chapter that brings beneficial changes to your world. It's a journey that captures the essence of self-development. It does direct your attention towards an endeavor that inspires and delights your mind. It culminates in an active and productive chapter. Watch the news that brings a boost to your life.

12 Wednesday

Flexing your adaptability muscle triggers a positive change that lets you unpack an exciting chapter that takes your vision to a new level. It does bring people into your life for a reason. As you expand your circle of friends, you can embrace a more connected and supportive environment. It leads to a busy and active chapter. A purposeful push gets you on the right path.

13 Thursday

The path ahead shines like diamonds; it does see a journey forward that brings an enriching chapter to the forefront of your life. It brings options, and this lets you proceed mindfully and with a plan in place. It brings a shift forward and offers a chance to develop a bond that draws excitement into your life. It does open the door, showing your intent and interest to this person opens the floodgates.

14 Friday ~ Sun sextile Uranus 23:02

In sextile with the Sun, Uranus captures the essence of surprises, new information, and discoveries. Something new and exciting is ready to manifest in your life. Being open to new people and possibilities charts a course towards rising prospects. It's an excellent time to explore a wider world of potential. Moving out of your comfort zone draws a spontaneous chapter that resonates beautifully with your vision.

15 Saturday

A stroke of luck arrives to position you on the correct path. It translates to a more prosperous journey; it does bring potential that offers room to grow your life. Changes ahead bring happiness. It is a time that lets you embrace a social environment that provides harmony and entertainment. It is a good time for helping others and offering guidance and support.

16 Sunday

An invitation arrives to tempt you to engage with your social life. It does bring a time of connecting with those who energize and enliven your life. A boost comes soon that offers you an unexpected opportunity. It is a phase of creativity, expansion, and abundance in your social life. It brings steady progress that highlights improving family life and personal ties.

17 Monday ~ Mercury square Jupiter 12:48, New Moon in Cancer 18:32

The power of intention is essential as planting seeds that bring inspiration and creativity to the forefront of your life. Something you become involved with is a catalyst for change and growth. It brings changes that expose confidential information. It helps you discover a path forward towards growing your life. It lets you pass the threshold and cross the bridge to a brighter future ahead.

18 Tuesday ~ Islamic New Year

You chart a course towards developing your vision. It generates excitement and progression as it offers an efficient and effective phase of growing your goals. It brings productivity, busyness, and expansion. Focusing on everyday tasks draws stability into your world. Resourceful planning helps you plot a course towards growth.

19 Wednesday

A time of personal growth ahead that draws soul-expanding experiences. It provides insight and clarity into the direction onward. Indeed, something inspirational flows into your world and gives you plenty of smiles. It touches you down on a chapter that offers change and growth. It brings ample time for transformation and new adventures. Making yourself a priority is essential.

20 Thursday ~ Sun trine Neptune 13:06, Mars opposed Saturn 20:39

The Sun trine Neptune alignment raises the vibration around your life. It focuses on improving the circumstances in your life and helping others who face difficult circumstances. Creativity is a valuable resource that lets you craft plans that offer tangible impacts that enhance your world.

21 Friday

Your life symbolizes fullness and fertility; it brings new possibilities to work with your skills. It gives you a leg up to a landscape that offers learning, growth, and wisdom. Reshaping your life lets you move in alignment with the person you are becoming. It gives you a chance to reinvent yourself and enjoy more freedom.

22 Saturday ~ Sun opposed Pluto 3:52

The Sun shines a light on a hidden aspect Pluto keeps out of sight in your day-to-day life. This opposition Pluto creates a doorway through which pockets of the inner self, spirit, and primal energy can reach the surface of your awareness. It shines a light on subconscious desires and instincts. Life has an edgier aspect that can feel unsettling today. It does get you in touch with hidden depths that spark an internal dialogue as you reveal a personal element of your personality.

23 Sunday ~ Venus turns Retrograde in Leo 1:33, Sun ingress Leo 1:47

Venus turns retrograde, which slows the progress down around your love life. Romantic development slows down or stagnates during this phase. Focus on the building blocks as the journey is as important as the final destination. If things feel stale in your love life, focus on creative areas and know that things will shift forward when Venus turns direct once more.

24 Monday

Something you have worked very hard toward reaches the pinnacle. It gets you rolling forward by fuelling the fire of your inspiration. You begin an entirely new cycle of growth. This next phase of progression lasts for the rest of this year. Your unique gifts and talents help achieve a robust result. It links you to positive change. Laying the groundwork one brick at a time draws a substantial influence.

25 Tuesday ~ First Quarter Moon in Libra 22:06

Favorable information arrives that advances your goals. It is a productive time that plants the seeds for future growth. It lets you maneuver forward and embrace developing your vision per your strategic plan for the future. It is a landscape that offers new adventures and improves your sense of well-being and harmony. It brings expansion on several levels, and this is a wonderfully creative aspect that provides room to grow your world.

26 Wednesday

The new information ahead lets something special into your life. It brings a project that becomes a jewel in your crown and replenishes your emotional tank. Scheduling time to focus on areas that capture your interest is a secret that rules a chapter of abundance. Sweet opportunities flow into your world to tempt you forward.

27 Thursday ~ Mercury conjunct Venus 15:15

The Mercury conjunct Venus aspect today bodes well for your personal life. Communication flows, as does feelings, emotions, and sentiments. The time is right to share loving thoughts and receive positive feedback from someone who holds meaning in your life. Insightful conversations crack the code to nurturing well-being and harmony in your life.

28 Friday ~ Delta Aquarids Meteor Shower. July 12th – August 23rd, Mercury ingress Virgo 21:29

Your drive to achieve your quest draws dividends. It lets you make progress on a chapter of personal growth. You connect with the one who supports your dreams and plays an important factor in future events. It lets you nurture a bond that offers room to grow into a significant path forward. A collaboration ahead brings a valuable sense of kinship.

29 Saturday

The timing is perfect for expanding your social life. It brings communication that elevates the potential possible. The conditions are improving, and this leads to invitations out. It lets you initiate expanding your horizons; this moves you away from tension and directs your energy towards a path that brings joy. Something of personal importance comes to light that brings a boost to your spirit.

30 Sunday

You enter a time of fortune and good luck. It reveals a significant change is possible. It brings a growth phase and an active transition to a busy and productive environment. An endeavor you participate in with friends draws a positive aspect. You may decide to branch out into a new area and explore a side project favoring growth and learning. It brings a windfall of potential.

AUGUST

Sun	Mon	Tue	Wed	Thu	Fri	Sat
		1	2	3	4	5
6	7	8	9	10	11	12
13	14	15	16	17	18	19
20	21	22	23	24	25	26
27	28	29	30	31		

New Moon

STURGEON MOON

31 Monday

You benefit from a new chapter that opens in your book of life. It puts you in touch with options that help you pass the threshold towards growing your world. It brings the kind of potential that reboots and rejuvenates your life from the ground up. There is a focus on working with your creativity that gets you in touch with hobbies. It ushers in new adventures that inspire and nurture your artistic side.

1 Tuesday ~ Lammas/Lughnasadh, Super Moon,
Sturgeon Full Moon in Aquarius 18:32, Mars trine Jupiter 20:44

A time of self-discovery ahead helps you gain insights into areas best released. It also allows you to discover pathways that offer a ray of sunshine. Intuitive choices bring new possibilities into your life. Getting involved in creating a life of your making helps smooth over the rough edges and lets you set sail towards smoother sailing.

2 Wednesday ~ Mercury opposed Saturn 2:16

As Mercury opposes Saturn, it brings heavy vibes into your life. The air of tension leaves a palpable sense of negativity around conversations and communication today. A serious-minded person may seek to have a strongly worded conversation with you. Setting boundaries creating space to nurture the foundations in your life helps restore balance if talks become pessimistic today. Pushing business decisions off for another day is advisable.

3 Thursday

Opening your life to new experiences draws dividends. It puts you in touch with a direction that holds promise. Investing in your life grows your vision for future growth. Setting intentions helps manifest goals and improves the energy surrounding your life. It is a potent time to create space to embrace the new potential. Contemplating your options enables you to navigate correctly and head towards an abundant landscape.

4 Friday

Sweeping changes are on the horizon as a new adventure calls your name. Complications fade away, and removing the outworn energy creates space to focus on an enterprising area. You get the wind back in your sails and embark on a journey that speaks to your heart. It brings a happier chapter that broadens your social circle.

5 Saturday

Your life lights up with new potential. It does see a fire of romance burning brightly in your life. You receive communication that tempts you towards change. Your life is a whirlwind of fun adventures. You are on the right path to a more connected future. It gets a welcome boost as growth moves into your social life. It kicks off a journey that draws improvement and nurtures a clear path forward.

6 Sunday

Dreaming about the future is a richly creative process that puts you in sync with a path of evolution and advancement. As you strive to move ahead, you reach a crossroads; taking time to think of imaginative solutions lets you chart a course towards growing your life. It helps you sail above life's issues by being open to change and adjusting the path accordingly.

7 Monday ~ Sun square Jupiter 12:03

Today's Sun square Jupiter aspect raises confidence and brings good fortune swirling around your life. It does boost your ego, which could lead to you overstepping the mark. Knowing your capabilities and working within the systems you have in place for your life will help keep things in check during this energetic time.

8 Tuesday ~ Last Quarter Moon in Taurus 10:48

Opportunity comes knocking and transitions you towards a journey that kicks off new options in your life. It helps you cut away from areas that are no longer relevant and move forward towards nurturing new goals and dreams. Creating space to plan for future growth brings potential into your life. Developments arise that bring sweet news into your life. It leads to an engaging time shared with friends.

9 Wednesday ~ Venus square Uranus 11:09

A surprise element adds a sense of uncertainty to your personal/social life due to the Venus square Uranus aspect today. A social vibe lands you in an environment ripe with refreshing options ready to blossom. It lets you make strides towards improving your life by expanding your circle of friends. Honing in on the potential brings happiness and joy. New goals emerge as you head towards a time that holds great promise.

10 Thursday ~ Mercury at Greatest Elongation 27.4 E, Mercury trine Jupiter 12:45

Mercury trine Jupiter today brings a boost into your life. Jupiter is the planet of good luck and fortuitous happenings, which improves the potential possible around your circumstances. It opens a window of opportunity that brings blessings into your world. You head towards a productive chapter that lays stable foundations. It brings a focus on improving the circumstances of your daily routines. It opens the floodgates towards new possibilities.

11 Friday

Momentum gathers as you redefine your life's constructs by being open and flexible to new people and environments. It lets you gain a deeper understanding of your natural strengths and talents. Renewal and rejuvenation is a theme that resonates in your world as you connect with friends who offer a supportive vibe. Life moves towards a social aspect that brings a vibrant landscape to explore.

12 Saturday ~ Perseids Meteor Shower July 17th - Aug 24th

Today brings a social aspect that harmonizes well-being and supports growth. It offers the prospects of developing a heart bond, which inspires change. It brings a dynamic change of pace that nurtures a supportive environment. Things fall into place, bringing space to renew your spirit from the ground up. It brings a path of happiness into focus that reboots and rejuvenates your energy.

13 Sunday

Adopting a broader perspective holds the key to rebalancing your energy. Information arrives that shines a light on improving the situation. It helps you turn a corner and draw peace and stability into your foundations. Letting fixed expectations help you move beyond areas that limit progress. It creates space for new goals and possibilities to emerge. It enables you to break down the hurdles and dive into an empowering phase of new options.

14 Monday

New opportunities prompt you to change your perception and approach. Reinventing your situation lets you blaze a way forward. A new trail has you gather momentum; it brings a creative path that enables you to harness your imagination to stunning effect. You overcome challenges with innovative insights and ideas. It does stir up the pot of manifestation, which lets you create magic ahead.

15 Tuesday

An opportunity emerges that opens a path forward to strengthen your ability to improve your circumstances. Essential changes inspire a great deal of growth. You head to an extensive chapter that reinvents the potential and brings a time of transition into your life. It allows your talents to shine, and it brings a purposeful and driven path that advances and refines your abilities. You extend your reach into a new area that offers growth and prosperity.

16 Wednesday ~ Sun square Uranus 2:34, New Moon in Leo 09:37, Mars trine Uranus 13:53

Uranus steals the show today, and you can expect a spontaneous and expressive environment that offers a breath of fresh air in your life. A change of scenery is on the horizon that brings a healing factor to your foundations. It leads to curious and adventurous time spent with friends. It relieves cabin fever and liberates your spirit with a sense of refreshing wanderlust.

17 Thursday

A positive trend is ready to burst into your life. It brings a busy time of new assignments, which drive growth to a new level. Riding a wave of advancing outcomes, you launch into developing your vision for future growth. New ideas and concepts flow freely into your life. A new project takes shape, bringing an enterprising time that sees you tackling a challenging aspect with relish.

18 Friday

You dial down on an area that provides abundance, companionship, and collaboration. Your carefree, curious nature craves a connection with like-minded individuals. It does bring a time of new experiences and moving out of your familiar groove by expanding your circle of friends. It brings a time of adventure and inspiration. It does have you dreaming big about future possibilities and planning for future growth.

19 Saturday

Good news offers curious benefits as it expands your circle of friends. You discover hidden advantages by expanding horizons and being open to new people and situations. Socializing with your broader circle of friends draws a new companion into your world. A positive influence looms overhead, bringing welcome news to your door.

20 Sunday

Today brings an emphasis on building stable foundations and nurturing your home life. It links you up to a chapter where you feel valued and appreciated. New possibilities are arriving soon, which lets you forge a trailblazing path towards developing your goals. It does bring a focused determination, which helps you improve your life through your willingness to work on your vision until you reach your destination.

21 Monday

An array of opportunities and pleasant surprises land in your lap soon. It connects you to a fresh start that nurtures your emotional wellness. You discover the pace and rhythm of life become active and dynamic. It sends a clear message that things are on the move. It draws bustling and productive options that see you progress in developing a dream. You touch down on some refreshing options that open the floodgates towards growing your abilities.

22 Tuesday ~ Venus square Jupiter 12:13, Mars opposed Neptune 20:33

A Venus Jupiter square offers rising prospects for your social life. You will have trouble concentrating on the task at hand as fun moments capture your attention. You make strides forward on making friends and sharing thoughts and ideas with others. It brings a fruitful time that sees your social life shining brightly. Mingling with a crew of entertaining characters does begin a fresh chapter that inspires you a great deal.

23 Wednesday ~ Sun ingress Virgo 8:58, Mercury turns retrograde 19:59

Mercury turns retrograde and puts a damper on the potential possible in your social life. It can cause miscommunication and issues in your love life. Mercury in retrograde adds an element that turns communication haywire. It disrupts the positive flow of energy in your life. Delay signing contracts or committing to business deals during a retrograde phase. It is an appropriate time for planning, but launch new endeavors after the retrograde cycle completes.

24 Thursday ~ First Quarter Moon in Sagittarius 9:57

You are ready to make great tracks on achieving a personal vision. It is a time that brings options for you to contemplate. Surrounding yourself with the right type of energy creates an abundant landscape that lets you move forward. Growth is possible; care and attention to detail draw rewards. The wheels are in motion; developments arise that tempt you forward.

25 Friday ~ Mars trine Pluto 12:22

Today's aspect offers rising prospects for your career. It brings a goal-orientated, disciplined, and centered focus on improving your working life. New options provide pathways that cultivate the refinement of skills. A breakthrough strategy offers a step up to advancing your life into a prestigious area. Changes ahead remove limiting factors as the essence of manifestation weaves magic around your life.

26 Saturday

Clearing away the cobwebs lets you create a clean sweep that nurtures these refreshing possibilities. Research and strategy are valuable companions that help you plot a course forward towards a lofty goal. It takes life to a new level as you forge ahead towards a unique endeavor. News arrives that highlights a little worn path toward a dream destination. A focus on self-development brings personal growth to the forefront of your life.

27 Sunday ~ Sun opposed Saturn 8:28, Mars ingress Libra r 13:15

Greener pastures, call your name soon. A new area beckons and offers curious benefits when developed. It gives you the green light to connect with inspiration and broaden the circle around your life. It draws friends and companions into your world, and that brings welcome news flowing into your life. It gives you a joyous snapshot of a lively chapter of personal growth. It brings sterling opportunities to mingle and network with a tribe of kindred spirits.

28 Monday

Life becomes brighter and greener as new opportunities beckon and tempt you forward. Being open to change and expansion sweetens the journey ahead. It captures the essence of wanderlust as you merge your dreams with a path that nurtures your spirit on many levels. It lets you make headway on developing your life. Investing your energy in promoting grounded foundations brings a journey of self-development and growth.

29 Tuesday ~ Uranus turns Retrograde in Taurus 2:11

Uranus moving into a retrograde phase boosts idealism; it offers big sky pictures that help motivate change to improve the world around you. This planetary cycle will boost your confidence and foster leadership qualities. It deepens initiative and offers a fresh wind that spurs creativity and an uptick of potential. It keeps inspiration humming along, and this heightens creativity. It brings solutions, pathways, and options ahead.

30 Wednesday

Being ready to open a new chapter in your book of life lets you snag a choice opportunity when a unique direction calls your name. It brings the stepping stones that expand your world while implementing essential strategies that encourage a stable base. It brings a grounded foundation that lets you light up new pathways when curious information sparks your interest.

31 Thursday ~ Super Moon, Blue Full Moon in Pisces 1:36

Taking a moment to process any unresolved emotions that could be lingering around your energy draws pleasing results. It speaks of a choice ahead that marks the transition towards a happy chapter. Being in a more social environment resonates wonderfully with your spirit. It does bring stability and consistency into your life. It draws a situation that has you exploring fresh ideas and engaging in entertaining discussions.

SEPTEMBER

Sun	Mon	Tue	Wed	Thu	Fri	Sat
					1	2
3	4	5	6	7	8	9
10	11	12	13	14	15	16
17	18	19	20	21	22	23
24	25	26	27	28	29	30

wild
SOUL

New Moon

CORN/HARVEST MOON

1 Friday

New opportunities ahead support expansion. It leads to an extensive chapter that reinvents the potential possible in your world. Excitement and possibility run rife through this enterprising time. It helps you gain a foothold on a brighter branch that offers robust options for your life. It brings a refreshing change of pace that grows creativity and enables you to develop innovative solutions to grow your world outwardly.

2 Saturday

You soon have many options on the table worth investigating. It brings a gratifying aspect that helps you enjoy smooth sailing. Life begins to feel soft and breezy again. It brings a social element that is supportive and harmonious. A vital phase begins rebuilding foundations and improving the outlook ahead.

3 Sunday

You are on track to improve your life. It suggests that a surprise crops up that rocks your world for the better. The tide turns in your favor as you enjoy lighter overtones that bring grace and expansion into your surroundings. It brings information that bolsters your mood and adds fun to your world. An emphasis on growing your life draws a social aspect that entices change.

4 Monday ~ Labor Day, Venus turns direct in Leo 1:19,
Mercury trine Jupiter 10:29, Jupiter turns Retrograde in Taurus 14:14

Venus turns direct and brings a positive influence that strengthens foundations. It creates space to nurture a time of fun, leisure, creativity, and social engagement. A strong emphasis on home and family life brings forward-facing momentum and lighter energy. You benefit from an extended time that offers curious assignments and endeavors.

5 Tuesday

The time is right to chase your dreams. Exploring new pathways transforms potential around your life. It brings a new level of understanding that focuses on the growth and refinement of skills and abilities. It heightens creativity as you learn to use your inherent gifts to grow your world and advance life towards greener pastures. Indeed, you unearth information that offers an avenue of interest.

6 Wednesday ~ Sun conjunct Mercury 11: 08, Last Quarter Moon in Gemini 22:21

Independent thinking and innovative ideas can be attributed to the Sun, Mercury conjunct today. It shapes up to be a productive time with lots of opportunities to explore. In short, things hum along, and you begin to see projects taking shape. Information arrives that is a boost for your spirits. It brings an expansive aspect that offers a lift as it beautifully supports your life.

7 Thursday

A new option ahead anchors your energy in an enterprising area. It brings a win-win situation into view, which favors expansion. As you shape the course onward, you discover new avenues that grow your talents. It opens the floodgates to a dynamic and active environment that hones your skills and refines your abilities. Nurturing your gifts brings a grounded foundation that provides stability as you grow your world.

8 Friday ~ Sun trine Jupiter 11:12

The Sun forms a trine with Jupiter, which increases good luck and fortune in your life. A positive influence creates the right environment for life to flow easily towards new goals. It brings a project to channel excess energy into development. Working with your abilities offers new pathways of growth and creativity that secure a great chapter ahead. It provides a social aspect that connects you with a broader tribe.

9 Saturday

A social environment brings a positive aspect into your life. Expanding options see you circulating with friends and kindred spirits. It draws a gentle element that offers rich rewards for your mood. Rising creativity surrounds this phase and beautifully accents your life with new ideas and options. It sparks a revolution that lets you unpack new possibilities with relish.

10 Sunday

As you chart a course towards developing your life, you enter a bountiful time of increasing potential around your home, social, and family life. It lets you focus on areas that hold the most significant meaning. It offers a unique perspective that rejuvenates your surroundings. Opening your mind to new possibilities and experiences expands your life outwardly. It brings a breakthrough that opens the gate to a dynamic chapter of growth.

11 Monday

Small changes can create extensive pathways towards growth. Look for signs and serendipity that help your dreams take flight. Developing your vision draws momentum and progress into your life. Your goals take shape, and you soon discover an open road of exciting options that tempt you forward. It marks the type of journey that redefines what is possible in your world when you allow your creativity to bloom.

12 Tuesday

You can prioritize achieving the highest result in your world. Being selective raises the bar and enables the better potential to emerge in your life. A strong emphasis on improving your situation cultivates lighter energy that breaks up stagnant patterns. It removes the blocks that limit progress and enable you to get busy developing your world from the ground up.

13 Wednesday

A change of pace arrives that offers remarkable change when news emerges that draws a boost. You discover several opportunities swirling around your social life that tempt you towards growing your world outwardly. It brings a lively and dynamic environment that offers activities and sharing with friends. It marks an excellent time for channeling your excess energy into developing new goals and endeavors.

14 Thursday

Exploring diverse options supports a journey of growth and evolution. It lets you land in a productive atmosphere that is ripe with potential. Opportunities to mingle set the scene to expand your social life with new friends and companions. It brings a happy chapter that rules a time of expansion and harmony. It brings thoughtful discussions that offer cutting-edge ideas, which blaze a trail towards a path of inspiration.

15 Friday ~ Rosh Hashanah (begins at sunset), New Moon in Virgo 1:40, Mercury turns direct 20:20

Mercury turns direct, and this improves communication and interpersonal bonds. It offers a renewed interest in your social life that helps harmonize frazzled tensions that occurred during the retrograde phase. Lively discussions and constructive dialogues paint a broader picture of what is possible in your life when you link up with other creative characters.

16 Saturday ~ Sun trine Uranus 1:23

The Sun trine Uranus aspect today adds a dash of spontaneity and excitement into your life. It is a favorable aspect that brings the freedom-driven chapter to light. Focusing on your social life draws a pleasing result as you connect with kindred spirits who offer excitement and passion. Creativity heightens, bringing experimental energy that provides the spice of life. You glide into a graceful time of socializing with friends.

17 Sunday ~ Rosh Hashanah (ends at sunset), Venus square Jupiter 6:12

The Venus square Jupiter aspect makes it the perfect day for unwinding and relaxing with your social circle. An easy-going vibe draws thoughtful conversations and entertaining ideas. It brings options into your world that is a cause for celebration. You get a chance to catch up with friends and mingle with kindred spirits. It draws sunny skies overhead that brings a boost to your mood.

18 Monday

Exploring various avenues helps advance your life. It initiates growth and change that has you feeling productive and active. Taking inventory helps plan the steps. Your willingness to sift and sort through ideas and pathways enables you to spot a rare and precious path that lights up with refreshing potential. You land in an ideal position to progress a goal forward. Perceived limitations fade away as an opportunity comes knocking.

19 Tuesday ~ Sun opposed Neptune 11:17

Your perception broadens as the Sun lights up Neptune's dreamy aspects. Engaging with creativity and imagination draws rising ideas and innovative concepts to consider. Life is ripe with potential ready to blossom in your world. It lets you remove the drama and release outdated areas that no longer hold interest in your life. News ahead unlocks essential information that clears the path forward. Life becomes more socially connected and enriching. It brings a fun and playful time that links you with social opportunities.

20 Wednesday

A new trend brings opportunities ahead. It lets you make effective changes that improve the stability and support in your world. Inspirational vibrations draw lighter energy, bringing an influx of creative ideas. Having practical solutions at your disposal places you in a solid position to improve your bottom line. Grounded foundations bring growth and progress. It draws a warm and enriching time that offers substantial benefits.

21 Thursday ~ International Day of Peace, Sun trine Pluto 5:20

A valuable breakthrough ahead creates space for new abundance to emerge in your life. It lets you hit your groove with a new routine that offers remarkable change. Imagination ignites inspiration and creativity. A lightbulb moment helps develop a dream area. It hooks you up with other people who form a soul tribe of connection around your social life.

22 Friday ~ Sun ingress Libra 6:46, First Quarter Moon in Sagittarius 19:32, Mercury at Greatest Elongation 17.9W

Alchemy is brewing in the background of your life that brings new options. Refining and streamlining your life draws an effective and efficient path towards growing your world. It brings good fortune and improvement to your social life when a chance collaboration inspires growth and progression. It broadens your perception when you open your life to new people and experiences.

23 Saturday ~ Mabon/Fall Equinox 6:50

Taking inventory of your situation helps pinpoint areas for removal. It brings an optimistic phase that lets you make headway on planning for future growth. It opens the floodgates towards an enterprising avenue that brings an active and vibrant chapter of working towards your goals. It helps you sidestep roadblocks and open a path that offers progress and prosperity. It brings an energetic rhythm that is dynamic and inspired.

24 Sunday ~ Yom Kippur (begins at sunset)

You may find that not a lot is happening at once, but things move forward gradually at the correct pace for your circumstances. It brings a greater emphasis on home and family life; sharing thoughts and ideas with others brings harmony into your world. It has you feeling favorable winds flowing into your surroundings.

25 Monday ~ Yom Kippur (ends at sunset), Mercury trine Jupiter 12:12

Today's Mercury trine Jupiter aspect brings optimism and good news. Research, learning, study, and socializing are favored. This trine is ideal for formulating new plans and engaging in future-orientated brainstorming sessions. It's also the perfect time to sort and organize; from your office, workspace, closet, or even your whole life.

26 Tuesday

Nurturing your abilities takes you towards advancement. Indeed, learning and growth are ahead in your life. Focusing on developing your goals holds you in good stead as it offers side journeys to grow your world. New Horizons tempt you forward. Creating space to make your vision a priority draws abundance into your life. It helps you reawaken to the magic and possibility of growing your aspirations.

27 Wednesday

Your priorities are shifting; it brings a journey that develops your world. Your situation is transforming towards a busy and creative time working with your abilities. It helps you move away from areas that no longer inspire or hold water. Pouring your energy into a journey worth growing brings change that guides your progress forward. It governs a time of increasing stability that rules getting back to basics and working with your skills to advance life.

28 Thursday

Taking advantage of new potential puts you in the prime position to draw an influx of good fortune into your world. It leads towards developing hopes and dreams as an expansive arena comes into view. It offers a busy time that lets you move up the ladder of success. It marks a bold beginning that brings joy and harmony into view. An abundant mindset broadens the playing field and draws brainstorming sessions with kindred spirits. It gets an upgrade to your life that offers room to progress goals.

OCTOBER

Sun	Mon	Tue	Wed	Thu	Fri	Sat
1	2	3	4	5	6	7
8	9	10	11	12	13	14
15	16	17	18	19	20	21
22	23	24	25	26	27	28
29	30	31				

NEW MOON

HUNTERS MOON

29 Friday ~ Sukkot (begins at sunset), Super Moon, Corn Moon, Harvest Full Moon in Aries 9:58, Venus square Uranus 17:53

A restless vibe caused by a Venus Uranus square could undermine the security in your love life or the broader social environment if you are single. A freedom-loving vibration brings a need to be spontaneous and engage in unique adventures that change out the day-to-day routine of your life.

30 Saturday ~Mercury trine Uranus 16:56

Today's trine is perfect for using technology to keep life are supported and flowing in your social life. Communication is your passageway to a more connected social life. Being innovative and thinking outside the box connects you with diverse pathways of growth and expansion.

1 Sunday

A social aspect helps progress your life by bringing new options worth considering. It connects you with inspiring possibilities that let you enter uncharted waters and double up the fun with kindred spirits. An element of surprise brings excitement and spontaneity to your social life. It draws a bustling and active time of sharing thoughts and talking with friends.

2 Monday ~ Mercury opposed Neptune 3:34

The Mercury and Neptune opposition helps you communicate your ideas and thoughts today. However, You may find work challenging as rising creativity brings a desire to daydream. Choosing a new path is never easy, but information ahead helps clear the way; it lets you plot a course towards your vision. It is a significant time that allows you to accomplish a great deal in your career path.

3 Tuesday ~ Mercury trine Pluto 19:20

Life offers new possibilities that draw stability and balance into your world. It helps you navigate forward towards greener pastures. Making yourself a priority brings a turning point as it connects you to people who support your growth and evolution. It opens the door to revolution and renewal. The strength in your spirit offers the ability to push back barriers and create a bridge towards a brighter chapter. News ahead brings a powerful boost into your world.

4 Wednesday

A changing scene on the horizon brings new potential into your social life. It connects you with kindred spirits, creating space to focus on developing ambitious goals. It brings a happy chapter that broadens your social circle. Abundance flourishes as you reveal new information that brings exciting options to light. Good energy flows easily and naturally around your life.

5 Thursday ~ Mercury ingress Libra 12:06

Mercury can bring an indecisive vibe that causes stagnant energy. Procrastination can be an issue that delays progress in the workplace. Focusing on removing distractions and streamlining your environment can help mitigate the effect of this transit. You have the discipline to stick with goals and develop your life following your vision. An offshoot or side adventure comes calling soon and brings something worth building.

6 Friday ~ Sukkot (ends at sunset), Last Quarter Moon in Cancer 13:48

A social gathering ahead brings joy into your life. It offers a busy and productive chapter of social inclusion and mingling with friends and companions who draw well-being and happiness into your life. Constructive dialogues provide a thoughtful perspective. It helps you brew up a storm of potential ideas by socializing with kindred spirits. It provides a clear path towards developing new areas of interest. It highlights luck and good fortune flowing into your world.

7 Saturday ~ Draconids Meteor Shower. Oct 6-10

Harnessing the energy of forgiveness is a powerful tool to improve bonds and harmonize aspects of your social life. It turns the page on a brighter chapter that uses empathy and compassion to draw balance into your surroundings. Resonating forgiveness and kindness is a fantastic way to explore the energy that draws stability and balance into interpersonal bonds. It brings a journey that draws transformation and happiness.

8 Sunday

A social aspect ahead lifts the lid on new opportunities. It brings a busy time that offers a foundation worth growing. It will seem like you've opened the window and let the fresh air flow into your world. It brings a time that rules expansion, which carries plenty of opportunities to explore. Being open to new people and situations sweetens your journey.

**9 Monday ~ Thanksgiving Day (Canada), Indigenous People's Day,
Columbus Day, Mars square Pluto 1:04, Venus ingress Virgo 1:06**

News arrives that helps craft your vision for future growth. It begins a journey that advances your life towards new options. It marks a significant turning point that lets you take hold of the reins and take charge of developing your life. It brings a lovely boost as lighter energy offers heightened inspiration and motivation. Creativity rises, delivering a wellspring of possibilities.

10 Tuesday ~ Venus opposed Saturn 6:11, Pluto turns direct 11:43

Your career goes from strength to strength as you extend your reach into this prominent area. Any issues currently on the periphery of your working life are soon dispersed and put behind you. It brings rapid improvements and an environment that is active and productive. You get established in a dynamic area with room to grow your talents. Life becomes brighter as greener pastures beckon and tempt you onward.

11 Wednesday

News arrives that brings balance and harmony into your life. It brings a time of expansion, creativity, and adventure. Your ability to manifest positive outcomes heightens, revealing the heartening type of advancement. It enriches your world and gives you a clear indication you are free to follow your heart and grow your life outwardly. You better understand what happens when you set the bar higher as you plot your course forward.

12 Thursday ~ Mars ingress Scorpio 3:59

An aspect ahead brings the answers to your more critical life questions. It opens a path that lets you channel your energy into an area of interest. It brings an engaging social interaction and friendly banter that adds playful energy into your life. It does have you dreaming big about the possibilities when you open your life to new people and experiences. It brings an active environment of mingling that offers enriching energy.

13 Friday ~ Mars trine Saturn 12:28

The Mars trine Saturn aspect today boosts your working life. It enables you to gain traction on achieving a successful result. It puts the finishing touches on your working week as you meet deadlines with ease. This robust transit gives you the strength, ambition, and perseverance to take on the most complex tasks and complete them on time. Increased productivity and efficiency get the job done. Your self-discipline keeps you focused without being distracted or discouraged.

14 Saturday ~ New Moon in Libra 17:54, Annular Solar Eclipse 17:59

A fortunate trend arrives that blends beautifully with your aspirations for future growth. It lets you make strides in improving your circumstances and navigating the path ahead with efficiency and grace. It gives you the green light to connect with inspiration and creativity. A surprise arrives that bolsters your mood. It brings a new friendship to light and lets you become involved in mingling and socializing.

15 Sunday

Opportunity comes knocking soon. It brings a chapter of soul-stirring conversations shared with friends. It ushers in thoughtful discussions that balance bonds and enriches your spirit. It brings expansion to your circle of friends as a new companion pops into view. Expanding your vision brings options that remove the heaviness and let the light in your life. It marks a time that is inspired and adventurous.

16 Monday

News arrives that cracks the code to the path ahead. A sweet deal is on offer, bringing a sense of comfort and security. Resources improve, and this gives you scope to broaden your horizons. It brings many assignments that offer room to grow your abilities. You see a massive increase in your creativity, and this advances your talents to the next level. You explore a rich offering of possibilities that extend your reach into new areas.

17 Tuesday

Exploring different possibilities enables you to advance your life, giving you the highest chance of a successful result. You build the next chapter with rock-solid foundations. You discover a role that suits your talents and takes your abilities to the next level. You scoop the pool and nail a position that offers room for progression. It brings a positive new direction that sees you climbing the ladder onward.

18 Wednesday

Curious changes ahead lead to improving your circumstances. It sets the stage for a stable progression that lets you focus on priorities and streamline your environment to have things run more effectively and efficiently. You enjoy a lighter side of life that plants the seeds that blossom gently over the coming months. It brings a social aspect that draws harmony and balance into your surroundings.

19 Thursday

New ideas and options arrive soon. Many raw opportunities are ready to be molded into a journey of abundance; following your heart emphasizes improving your surroundings. Third, it launches a happy and dynamic social environment that blesses your world on several levels. Finally, it helps you build your social circle outwardly.

20 Friday ~ Sun conjunct Mercury 5:37

In conjunction with Mercury, the Sun is a favorable aspect that attracts communication. It is the best of all elements for receiving or sending communication. Interacting with others is vital today. It stimulates your need to share ideas and engage in thoughtful discussions that nurture well-being and harmony in your life.

21 Saturday ~ Orionids Meteor Shower Oct 2nd – Nov 7th,
Mercury square Pluto 12:50, Sun square Pluto 14:09

Today's aspect causes a challenging environment as you find your judgment or authority tested. Being challenged and put to the test feels uncomfortable as you think you are making the right choices and decisions for your life. The Mercury square Pluto transit also attracts interactions with other people who feed the gossip mill and cultivate drama, leading to a toxic environment.

22 Sunday ~ First Quarter Moon in Aquarius 03:29, Venus trine Jupiter 4:32,
Mercury ingress Scorpio 6:46, Mercury trine Saturn 16:12

The Venus trine Jupiter aspect offers golden threads around your social and love life. It is one of the most anticipated transits which harmonizes interpersonal bonds and offers rising prospects of good luck to your romantic life. It is of particular interest to those seeking love or lovers wanting a deeper romantic bond.

23 Monday ~ Venus at Greatest Elongation 46.4W, Sun ingress Scorpio 16:17

It is a favored time to take on new assignments. It lets you build your career path under a positive trend that sees you engaged with learning and growth. It brings discussions that open pathways that offer progression. It's not a quick fix, but you lay the groundwork methodically and securely.

24 Tuesday ~ Sun trine Saturn 7:13

Today's Sun, Saturn trine gives you a commanding presence in the workplace. Confidence peaks in mid-afternoon, enabling you to effectively manage the day's tasks with relative ease as your energy keeps humming along productively. You conquer the workload and achieve a robust result with your consistent and disciplined efforts, which draw a pleasing effect and the added benefits of increased job satisfaction.

25 Wednesday

There will be a side avenue ahead that calls your name and grow your abilities. Growth and learning are the basis from which you expand your life. Working with your talents refines your skills and enables you to develop a winning journey forward. Following the calling within your spirit is putting you in the proper alignment.

26 Thursday

A time of adventure and changing circumstances puts you in touch with the liberating sense of freedom as you cross the threshold towards a brighter future. Exploring areas that grow your world brings a remarkable turning point. It translates to a chapter that renews and rebuilds the foundations of your life. It brings a time of abundance that shines a light on possibilities that glimmer with gold.

27 Friday

Harnessing your ancestral power helps you achieve a robust result for your life. It is natural and reasonable to feel stressed as you contemplate an uncertain future, but allowing these feelings to arise and be released helps you maintain balance. It develops the strength to overcome challenges. Hurdles are simply an invitation to grow your spirit, and you will do just fine as you move forward in life.

28 Saturday ~ Mars opposed Jupiter 16: 03, Hunters Full Moon in Taurus 20:23 Partial Lunar Eclipse 20:14

You can embrace one of the luckiest opposition aspects today when Mars opposes Jupiter and draws good fortune into your life. The winds of change carry news information into your surroundings. Today's transit increases your self-confidence and ability to handle your time and energy demands. It brings a competitive edge that fuels ambitions and the desire to achieve your goals.

29 Sunday ~ Mercury opposed Jupiter 3:44, Mercury conjunct Mars 14:21

Today, Mercury is the show's star and draws a favorable aspect that nurtures good fortune in your social life. It brings a chance to share with friends and loved ones. Relaxing and unwinding enable you to restore frazzled nerves and build robust foundations.

November

Sun	Mon	Tue	Wed	Thu	Fri	Sat
			1	2	3	4
5	6	7	8	9	10	11
12	13	14	15	16	17	18
19	20	21	22	23	24	25
26	27	28	29	30		

New Moon

BEAVER MOON

30 Monday

There is a new beginning ahead for your life. Channeling the essence of forgiveness brings a journey towards a bright and abundant landscape. It reveals new friendships in a social environment that offers a chance to unwind and enjoy constructive conversations. It brings plenty to feel happy about as it draws a path you can cherish and progress. It brings excitement and adventure to the forefront of your life.

31 Tuesday ~ Samhain/Halloween, All Hallows Eve Venus trine Uranus 12:51

Embrace a magical and vibrant Halloween under the influence of an engaging and dynamic Venus trine Uranus aspect that adds a dash of spontaneity and fun into your life. Brainstorming sessions ensure you are engaging your creativity and nurturing your gifts. The more you dabble with life, the more new possibilities come to meet you.

1 Wednesday ~ All Saints' Day

The past has been a series of stepping stones that grew your world. You continue to draw opportunities for growth and learning into your life. The more you dabble with new possibilities, the more you reveal latent gifts and abilities. It connects you with the freedom to explore a journey that inspires your soul. It speaks of a positive flow-on effect that nurtures well-being when you listen to your heart.

2 Thursday

New opportunities get good news, heightening the chances that things are ready to head to an upswing. Creativity elevates; it connects you with a path that sparkles with possibility. You discover a venture that satisfies your yearning for adventure. It takes you towards a sunny destination. It has you feeling in sync with others on a similar trajectory. It brings discussions and ideas which flow freely with friends.

3 Friday ~ Sun opposed Jupiter 5:02. Venus opposed Neptune 22:05

The Sun opposed Jupiter transit brings the increasing potential for wealth and good fortune. Rising prospects see things in your life fall in place as you turn a corner and head towards a lucky streak. A decision ahead blends beautifully with future aspirations; it extends your reach further afield as you plot a course towards a lofty goal. It brings refinement to your core talents and elevates the potential possibilities for your career path.

4 Saturday ~ Taurids Meteor Shower. Sept 7th - Dec 10th
Saturn turns direct in Pisces 7:15. Mercury opposed Uranus 16:06

The Mercury opposed Uranus transit brings a chaotic and hectic pace. The busier pace may leave you feeling tense, anxious, and scattered. Uranus adds a dash of the unexpected, leaving you scrambling to deal with surprise news. Information emerges out of the left-field, leaving you wondering what will happen next. Focusing on the basics improves balance.

5 Sunday ~ Last Quarter Moon in Leo 08:37

News arrives that shines a light on a promising direction. It brings a highly supportive journey that gets a chance to unwind with friends. The expansion and joy that are looming overhead draw a pleasing result. Events align in your favor, and this connects you with a companion who nurtures your spirit. It gives you a solid base to grow your circle of friends. It offers a lovely time that hits a high note in your social life.

6 Monday ~ Venus trine Pluto 14:38

Today's Venus trine with Pluto adds intensity to your love life. This aspect turns up the heat in your personal life. Sexual attraction and passion rise as you get busy developing your personal life. Singles are likely to find new romance soon, while couples can embrace a more connected and sizzling love life.

7 Tuesday ~ Mercury trine Neptune 1:36

Creativity, imagination and innovation blaze a wildfire of inspiration as Mercury and Neptune form a trine today. Increased sensitivity to this vibrational energy attracts a boost into your world that bolsters vitality. It offers a dramatic shift that helps you quickly learn or develop a new area.

8 Wednesday ~ Venus ingress Libra 9:27

Life becomes a little lighter as you step out in a more social environment soon. Paying attention to the signs is a compelling call to action. Life brims with possibilities that help you make tracks towards improving your world. You strike gold by expanding your social circle as you turn the corner and enter a winning chapter of nurturing interpersonal bonds. It smooths over the rough edges of your life and brings companionship to your door.

9 Thursday ~ Mercury sextile Pluto 12:16

Today, the Mercury sextile Pluto transit adds extra layers and dimensions to your creative thinking. It brings an ideal time for research, planning, and mapping out unique areas for future development. Your penetrating inquiries delve deep and help you discover any potential pitfalls and issues. Your inquiring mind places you in a solid position to grow your dreams as you do due diligence and understand all aspects around your investigations.

10 Friday ~ Veterans Day (Observed), Mercury ingress Sagittarius 6:22, Mercury square Saturn 15:07

Today's Mercury square Saturn challenges critical thinking skills and intrepid enquiring. Tensions could flare up and lead to disruptions. Miscommunication is more likely when you are not on the same page as the person you talk to about your thoughts and ideas.

11 Saturday ~ Veterans Day, Remembrance Day (Canada), Mars opposed Uranus 21:11

The Mars opposed Uranus could catch you off guard today, leading to tension in personal bonds. An unexpected tension could flare up, causing an argument or dispute with a family member or loved one. Seeing the truth cuts through murky waters and draws clarity and insight into the path ahead. It helps process complicated emotions, and resolving past issues creates new potential.

12 Sunday

The changes ahead bring a time to shine. It lets you bid farewell to past issues that have blocked progress. It brings new possibilities that allow you to reach a turning point. An expansive landscape comes into view. It brings social opportunities that add richness to your life. It offers a powerful new beginning as it draws a fresh start into your social life. Lively conversations fuel a desire for expansion.

13 Monday ~ New Moon in Scorpio 09:27, Sun opposed Uranus 17:20

The Sun opposed Uranus transit attracts a restless vibe that gives you the green light to try something new and different. It drives a liberating chapter that offers spontaneity as you get busy expressing your unique individual melody and personality. News arrives that delivers a boost to your morale. It places you in the correct alignment to progress your vision when a sunny aspect flings open the door to a new chapter.

14 Tuesday

You are drawing a path that moves you in alignment with your dreams. A choice is made directly from the heart. It brings an abundant chapter with edgy new energy swirling around your environment. It does let you create tracks on your journey; change arrives, it sees things moving forward with the trajectory speaks to your soul. It gives you a better understanding of where you are going and how to get there.

15 Wednesday ~ Mercury sextile Venus 12:47

A loving vibe helps you get past hump day. Today's Mercury sextile Venus adds a positive influence that harmonizes and nurtures well-being in your world. Less stress and more enjoyment grow solid foundations. Personal relationships benefit from open communication leading to fulfillment. It does shine a light on support and conversations that create space for abundance to flow into your life. It brings a boost to your creativity, and this could spark a new path forward.

16 Thursday

Reinvention is a strong theme for your life at this time. An element of change brings restructuring that lets you sift through your options and bring goodness to the top of the pile. It provides steady progress towards developing foundations that offer security and a solid basis for growing your life. It is a gateway that opens towards a happy chapter where you achieve active progression on your vision.

17 Friday ~ Leonids Meteor Shower November 6-30th, Mars trine Neptune 8:36, Sun trine Neptune 14:51

Under the influence of Neptune, creativity soars, epiphany's, and lightbulb moments are the order of the day. It creates a grounded basis and enables you to feel able to progress skills. You can elevate your potential and reach for a new level of evolution. Your career path is on a trajectory that draws new options.

18 Saturday ~ Sun conjunct Mars 5:41

Sun conjunct Mars brings an abundance of energy and initiative, your drive to try new things increases. A desire for action can cause restlessness if not channeled and released. A whirlwind of activity ahead draws new options into your life. It brings a time of expanding horizons that draw several crosscurrents through your social life. It encourages community participation and offers a lively and dynamic sharing chapter with friends and companions. Lighting a path towards a social aspect draws well-being and harmony into your world.

19 Sunday

Waiting for information, you engage in original thinking that helps manifest the magic needed to embark on your next phase of life. It is a necessary time to allow your creative ideas to bubble up to the surface. Your original expression amplifies the potential available in your life. It brings an endeavor that draws excitement.

20 Monday ~ First Quarter Moon in Aquarius 10:50, Sun sextile Pluto 21:26

Today's Sun sextile Pluto transit drives ambitions and sees you heading into the working week with an increased drive to succeed and conquer your goals. Feeling determined and purposeful enables you to nail your tasks quickly and finish work with energy still in the tank. It leads to a busy time that sees headway around your larger goals. Today blossoms into a journey of purpose and happiness as you gain traction on achieving a pleasing result for your life.

21 Tuesday

Experimenting and exploring pathways brings the ideal amount of spice and excitement into your life. You flavor your world with an enticing mix of potential that lets you move forward towards a fresh start. It sees you becoming more assertive about what you seek and taking steps to reach for your vision. Rapid improvements draw an environment that is active and productive.

22 Wednesday ~ Mars sextile Pluto 1:17, Sun ingress Sagittarius 13:59

Today's transit increases energy in the workplace. No job is too small as you take on the lot and work towards your vision. Information arrives that is a catalyst for growth. It rules using your talents to forge an enterprising trail towards your dreams. It shines a light on what you can achieve when you keep your mind open to new avenues. A theme of improving circumstances enables you to adapt to the changing environment ahead.

23 Thursday ~ Thanksgiving Day (USA), Sun square Saturn 9:46

Saturn is the ruler of honoring traditions and following rigid structures that form set boundaries. Today's square illuminates a happy time shared with loved ones, perfect with Saturn, who delights in honoring the past. The past has been a challenging time that grew your life in many ways. It has shaped the person you are today; being flexible, understanding, and compassionate brings new opportunities into your world. It harmonizes life on many levels.

24 Friday ~ Mars ingress Sagittarius 10:10

This transit emits a rebellious vibe that rejuvenates your energy and has you seeking expansion. You may feel an irresistible urge to explore new pathways. Nothing holds you back from growing your life; it feels liberating, expansive, and exciting. It brings a fantastic time to share your talents and develop your abilities in a new area. It lets you find your groove as you embark on improving your world.

25 Saturday ~ Mars square Saturn 16:57

Today's aspect can feel challenging as your mind is on Saturn's to-do list. Lifting the lid on a fresh chapter, see the fires of your inspiration and creativity burning brightly. It lets you make headway on achieving progress. It links you with expanding horizons that offer refreshing momentum and progress in your life. You cultivate goals with an area that captures your attention.

26 Sunday

Deep reflection, and contemplation, are valuable tools that encourage balance in your world. It helps you push through towards a brighter chapter; it triggers developments that offer a significant life shift forward. It ushers in new potential as you gain insight into your future life direction. Investigating leads soon points you in the right direction and brings a journey that offers growth and self-development. It brings changes that advance life spiritually and creatively.

27 Monday ~ Beaver Full Moon in Gemini 09:16, Mercury square Neptune 13:26

Today, the Mercury square Neptune aspect can distort or make mountains of molehills. It adds a dash of illusion into your business dealings that can have your head spinning with tall tales and trying to sort the truth from the exaggeration. Doing research will help answer any concerns you may have in your life. It gives you a clear and concise path forward that nurtures well-being in your world.

28 Tuesday

Becoming involved with growing your life brings progress and optimism into your world. It creates a stable foundation that illuminates new possibilities that help you craft your vision for future growth. As you journey towards developing a long-held goal, you begin to feel more hopeful about the rising prospects in your life. It helps you release the shadows and focus on meaningful areas that inspire your life and grow your abilities.

29 Wednesday

Opportunities ahead grow your world in new areas. It brings a positive side that offers a chance to nurture your talents in a creative environment. Sparkling vibrations of positivity flow into your life which helps support a journey of growth and evolution. A networking opportunity aligns your energy with kindred spirits. A new project offers fullness and abundance; it brings an exciting phase of nurturing your abilities and growing your skills.

30 Thursday

A path opens by surprise and offers advancement. It brings swift progression that enables you to raise the bar on what you thought was possible in your working life. New information draws an exciting possibility that places a strong emphasis on improving the security in your world. It offers an uptick of potential that becomes a source of prosperity and progress.

December

Sun	Mon	Tue	Wed	Thu	Fri	Sat
					1	2
3	4	5	6	7	8	9
10	11	12	13	14	15	16
17	18	19	20	21	22	23
24	25	26	27	28	29	30
31						

New Moon

COLD MOON

1 Friday ~ Mercury ingress Capricorn 14:29

It is a fruitful time to expand your network. Moving out of your comfort zone brings a highly productive cycle for your social life. It does bring new people into your life that ramps up the potential. It lets you create headway on creating stable foundations that support and nurture your goals. It connects you to a happy chapter that leaves you feeling appreciated.

2 Saturday ~ Mercury sextile Saturn 15:25

Today's Mercury sextile Saturn transit is favorable for organizing and streamlining your workload to create a stimulating and productive environment. Expressing authority and leadership skills create a purposeful and productive environment. It places you at a considerable advantage that marks the beginning of a shift forward towards your vision.

3 Sunday ~ Venus square Pluto 13:29

Today's aspect could see a flare-up of jealousy or possessiveness. Your romantic partner may feel threatened by heightened social activities and invitations in the pre-run up to Christmas. Take time to support and boost confidence to help offset the Venus square Pluto aspect. Being aware of these fears' dynamics helps keep relationships healthy and balanced.

4 Monday ~ Mercury at Greatest Elongation 21.3 E, Venus ingress Scorpio 18:48

News and invitations appear that brighten your mood. It shines a light on developing friendships and catching up with your broader circle of friends. You benefit greatly from a flurry of activity that surrounds your life. Nurturing foundations draws a wellspring of highly compatible options. It brings a purposeful and lively environment that sees things humming along nicely in your social life.

5 Tuesday ~ Last Quarter Moon in Virgo 05:50, Venus trine Saturn 22:51

Today's Venus trine Saturn transit is ideal for developing relationships. Self-expression, warmth, and affection flow freely under this favorable aspect. Taking time to configure your vision lets you move towards a chapter that holds new possibilities. New foundations bring an active phase of growth. It does guide you forward and help you achieve a robust result.

6 Wednesday ~ Neptune turns direct in Pisces, 12:38

With Neptune turning direct in Pisces, an extra emotional element adds flavor to your dreams, creativity, and vision. Wistful thinking, goals, and fantasies let you move beyond the material world and escape into fanciful thoughts around future possibilities. You may be waiting for your ship to come in and contemplating the options in your life. You achieve maximum results through your willingness to strategize and plan your goals.

7 Thursday ~ Hanukkah (begins at sunset)

It is a great time to appreciate all you have achieved. You can set your sights on developing your skills and abilities further. A significant change is on the horizon. It lets you unwrap a journey worth exploring. It brings the essential time for following your intuition and exploring pursuits that grow your talents. You open pathways towards growth that enable you to harness your adaptability and creativity.

8 Friday ~ Mercury trine Jupiter 4:04

Mercury's trine Jupiter transit today ignites the possibility of heightened intuition and attracts a chance to chill with friends. Getting involved with attending gatherings and connecting with your broader tribe nurtures harmony and well-being. It lets you share with people who support your ideas and plans. It brings an enterprising chapter that feeds creativity.

9 Saturday

A gathering ahead brings a reconnection with someone you haven't seen for a while. It offers an uplifting time that connects you with kindred spirits. You attract this person's attention and begin a path of sharing sentimental moments with someone who feels compatible with your life. Being in contact with one another once more draws lighter energy into your life.

10 Sunday ~ Venus opposed Jupiter 3:34

This astrological transit adds an indulgent vibration and has you wanting to explore hedonism, romance, and magic. The pursuit of pleasure attracts social engagement, relaxing, and unwinding with a leisurely influence restoring well-being in no time. It launches a time of developing goals that strongly focus on your family life.

11 Monday ~ Mercury sextile Venus 19:22

Communication flows freely into your social life, attracting invitations and opportunities to mingle. The Mercury sextile Venus aspect nurtures stable foundations and happiness. A surprise breakthrough draws new possibilities into your social life. It brings everything you need to feel happy and contented. It links with friends and brings social activities seamlessly into your world.

12 Tuesday ~ New Moon in Sagittarius 23:32

An opportunity in your local community lets you embrace a social environment. It brings you in contact with new characters it gives insight into new pathways of growth. It does help you spread your wings and map out new options. It does bring a rise in confidence; finding your feet in a new area is a soothing balm for your restless soul.

13 Wednesday ~ Mercury turns Retrograde in Capricorn 7:08
Geminids Meteor Shower Dec 7-17th

Mercury turns retrograde, seeing some communication issues cropping up over the next few weeks. Plans and times quickly become mixed as messages scramble during this more chaotic planetary phase. You can use this time wisely to think about the path ahead. Creativity and a curious mind combine to help you investigate new options that land you in an environment that is ripe for progression.

14 Thursday

There is more stability on offer; it does speak of a change that lets you dive into a social environment. It helps you embrace new options that support a chapter of growth. Social invitations bring moments to value. It is a fantastic time that sees things improving on the home front. It kicks off a path towards an exciting chapter that provides you with the right environment to thrive.

15 Friday ~ Hanukkah (ends at sunset)

A gateway ahead brings a journey of intrigue and adventure. It does help you come out on top. It ignites heightened potential for your personal life. This progression sets in motion a time that propels you towards developing a bond of interest. It helps you find your groove in a social environment that brings opportunities to network and communicate with others.

16 Saturday

New information ahead creates a positive shift forward for your life. Expect signs and serendipity that tempt you to try new avenues. A major topic of discussion opens a path worth growing with friends and companions. It brings an ideal time to circulate with your broader social environment and connect with others who support and nurture your world. It marks the beginning of an enriching journey forward.

17 Sunday

You touch down on a path that highlights potential and possibility. It brings self-discovery and personal growth to the forefront of your life. It initiates a stable phase of growing your world and opens a happier chapter. It provides a suitable avenue to increase your abilities. Something inspirational flows into your world and brings sunny skies overhead. Life expands as you focus on improving your circumstances. It brings magic and abundance into your world.

18 Monday ~ Mercury trine Jupiter 14:33

Mercury trine Jupiter transit brings optimism, luck, and good news. Information arrives that bodes well for your social life. Indeed, it's easy to make new friends under this favorable influence that sparks social engagement and thoughtful discussions with friendly characters. Mingling with your broader circle of friends opens your life to new people and experiences.

19 Tuesday ~ First Quarter Moon in Pisces 18:39

News and information emerge that helps you make good headway around developing new goals. You accomplish a great deal by being willing to grow your life outwardly. Change is coming; a potent mix of manifestation, inspiration, and creativity crack the code to a brighter chapter ahead. It sets the stage to establish a grounded foundation, and it offers expansion that has you exploring unique pathways ahead.

20 Wednesday

A social aspect ahead brings lightness into your life. It emphasizes improvement around your life that offers grounded foundations. A sense of manifestation that brings intriguing energy that helps you tap into the new potential. It brings an opportunity to join forces with someone who supports your world on many levels. It marks a time of positive communication that offers a social aspect ahead.

21 Thursday ~ Ursids Meteor Shower Dec 17th – 25th, Venus opposed Uranus 7:04, Mercury sextile Saturn 12:35

Today's Venus opposed Uranus alignment brings growth to personal relationships. Increasing synergy and chemistry could spark a new romance or flirtation opportunity. It brings a carefree and happy time that lets you relax and let your guard down with someone who captures your attention. It brings lively discussions with someone who shines brightly.

22 Friday ~ Sun ingress Capricorn 3:24, Yule/Winter Solstice 03:28, Sun conjunct Mercury 18:53

The Sun conjunct Mercury aspect favors communication. It brings the sharing of thoughtful dialogues and entertaining discussions. Notable changes ahead highlight a journey towards growing your social life. It brings a time of joyful possibilities that puts you in the box seat to cultivate your life. It connects you to a path that offers room to nurture latent abilities.

23 Saturday ~ Mercury ingress Sagittarius 6:19

Christmas brings a time of expansion that nurtures your life on many levels. It unlocks a chapter that transforms your world—a happy time spent collaborating with others who offer valuable guidance and ideas. It is a lovely time that draws enriching experiences and good fortune into your life. It opens the floodgates to a happier chapter that improves the potential possible in your life.

24 Sunday ~ Sun sextile Saturn 17:28

Sun sextile Saturn transit lends patience to family gatherings, which can be a godsend if your family dynamics tend to be challenging. A cornucopia of lighter energy creates a surge of opportunity for your social life. It brings choices and decisions that offer a bumper crop that revolutionizes the potential possible in your world. It reawakens you to a vibrant social aspect that removes the blocks.

25 Monday ~ Christmas Day, Venus trine Neptune 17:15

Venus trine Neptune transit is the perfect backdrop to Christmas. It attracts creativity, well-being, and fulfillment. This transit favors singing, music, and delighting in the celebration of the day. It brings a lively and happy time of sharing thoughts and discussions with those who support your world. The conditions are perfect for sharing and embracing a time of relaxation and rejuvenation. News arrives that brings sweet notes into your social life.

26 Tuesday ~ Kwanzaa begins

An invitation ahead brings a heartwarming phase into your life. It lays the foundations for an exciting time shared with kindred spirits. It takes you to a radiant chapter that offers gifts of self-expression and creativity. It sees the inspiration flowing into your life, restoring balance. It releases a social and freedom-loving chapter of connecting with friends.

**27 Wednesday ~ Cold Full Moon, Moon before Yule in Cancer 0:34,
Mercury square Neptune 7:36, Sun trine Jupiter 15:28**

The Sun trine Jupiter aspect lights up good fortune across the board. New possibilities blossom as a favorable wind ignites your passion and imagination. A fantastic boost arrives that helps you make exceptional progress on developing the path ahead. It brings positive energy and an encouraging vibe that offers room to grow your world.

28 Thursday ~ Mercury conjunct Mars 0:26, Mars square Neptune 22:15

The Mars square Neptune aspect brings gossip and scandal to your ears. You hear surprising news that feels disconcerting. Suppose something doesn't ring true to your ears. In that case, you should do your own investigating as this transit could draw misinformation leading to confusion.

29 Friday ~ Venus sextile Pluto 6:00, Venus ingress Sagittarius 20:21

The Venus sextile Pluto transit deepens romantic love and grows relationship potential. It brings an expressive time of nurturing a wellspring of abundance in your world. It does bring sentimentality to the forefront of your life. Feeling nostalgic is natural; focusing on your home life draws a nurturing and domestic side that offers bliss. It creates foundations that bring security. You can use this stability to turn a new page in your book of life.

30 Saturday

You reveal curious information that opens the gate to a fresh start in your life. It focuses on the essence of adventure as you connect with kindred spirits to brainstorm ideas and plan a strategy around future goals. It brings the chance to expand your circle of friends, and this companionship replenishes your emotional tank. It cultivates a therapeutic element that nourishes your soul on many levels.

31 Sunday ~ New Year's Eve, Jupiter turns direct in Taurus 2:41

In a promising sign, Jupiter turns direct on New Year's Eve. It foretells bright blessings, good fortune, and opportunities on the horizon. Unlimited possibilities spark inspiration as you begin a trailblazing journey towards improving your life. It does see a whirlwind of activity arriving that supports your growth. You benefit from this dynamic chapter; a dream comes into focus, blessing your life, and nurturing this goal becomes a focal point.

Astrology & Horoscope Books.

https://mystic-cat.com/

www.ingramcontent.com/pod-product-compliance
Lightning Source LLC
Chambersburg PA
CBHW080530090426
42733CB00015B/2538